I0477001

THE ORIGINS OF U.S. SOCIAL SECURITY PROGRAM PROBLEMS:
IMPLICATIONS FOR REFORM

NAPOLEON IMARHIAGBE, PhD

authorHOUSE®

AuthorHouse™
1663 Liberty Drive
Bloomington, IN 47403
www.authorhouse.com
Phone: 1 (800) 839-8640

© 2016 Napoleon Imarhiagbe, PhD. All rights reserved.

No part of this book may be reproduced, stored in a retrieval system, or transmitted by any means without the written permission of the author.

Published by AuthorHouse 05/26/2016

ISBN: 978-1-5049-7989-4 (sc)
ISBN: 978-1-5049-7988-7 (e)

Print information available on the last page.

Any people depicted in stock imagery provided by Thinkstock are models, and such images are being used for illustrative purposes only.
Certain stock imagery © Thinkstock.

This book is printed on acid-free paper.

Because of the dynamic nature of the Internet, any web addresses or links contained in this book may have changed since publication and may no longer be valid. The views expressed in this work are solely those of the author and do not necessarily reflect the views of the publisher, and the publisher hereby disclaims any responsibility for them.

CONTENTS

Acknowledgments	ix
Preface	xiii

PART 1: BREADTH COMPONENT — 1

INTRODUCTION	2
DEVELOPMENT OF SOCIAL SECURITY AROUND THE WORLD	3
SOCIAL SECURITY BEFORE THE GREAT DEPRESSION	5
ANALYZING SOCIAL SECURITY PROBLEMS	8
The Implications of the Burgeoning Elderly Population	9
THE SUSTAINABILITY OF THE U.S. SOCIAL SECURITY SYSTEM	10
Social Security: An Evolutionary Process	11
Benefits Paid by Social Security	12
The Growth of the Social Security Benefits and Taxes	13
Argument for the Reform of the Social Security Program	15
Social Security Reform and Democratic Governance	16
OTHER NATIONS' SOCIAL SECURITY REFORM MODELS	17
SOCIAL SECURITY RISKS VERSUS PRIVATE INVESTMENT RISKS	21
CONCLUSION	25

PART 2: THE DEPTH COMPONENT — 31

ANNOTATED BIBLIOGRAPHY	32
INTRODUCTION	41
SOCIAL SECURITY AND ELDERLY	42
POOR AND LOW-INCOME EARNERS	42
AFRICAN AMERICANS AND SOCIAL SECURITY	44
WOMEN AND SOCIAL SECURITY	44
PRIVATE INVESTMENT AND SOCIAL SOCIETY	46
CONCLUSION	47

PART 3: APPLICATION COMPONENT — 49
- INTRODUCTION — 50
- IMPLICATIONS OF THE MARKET SOLUTION — 52
- ADVANTAGES OF A MARKET SOLUTION — 53
- DISADVANTAGES OF THE NONMARKET SOLUTION — 54
- COMPARE AND CONTRAST — 54
- ALTERNATIVE PLANS TO SOCIAL SECURITY PRIVATIZATION — 55
    - Galveston County Alternative Plan to Social Security — 58
    - NYC Alternative Plan to Social Security Privatization — 59
- RECOMMENDATIONS — 60
- CONCLUSION — 63

PART 4: EMPIRICAL RESEARCH — 65
- EMPIRICAL RESEARCH RELATED TO THIS STUDY — 66

Bibliography — 69
Glossary — 93
Operational Definitions — 97

TRADEMARKS AND RIGHTS

Throughout this book, we refer to products and designs which are not our property. These references are meant only to be informational. We do not represent the companies mentioned and were not paid promotional fees. However, if these companies would like to send us evaluation copies of future products, we would be thrilled. References to products are not endorsements, but reflect our opinions in some cases.

Computer software products mentioned are the property of their respective publishers. Instead of attempting to list every software publisher and brand, or including trademark symbols throughout this book, we assume that you know these product and brand names are protected under U.S. and international laws. Fonts and designs are the intellectual property of the design artists. Although U.S. copyright laws do not protect font designs, we consider them the property of the designers and licensing agencies.

ACKNOWLEDGMENTS

First of all, I want to thank the almighty God for keeping me alive, so that I might have the opportunity to complete this book. As I understand it, everyone has a purpose to serve in life, and one of the greater opportunities for purposeful action is to write a book that potentially improves the well-being of others. A book aimed at improving government services or social services is a part of that greater purpose, a researcher's achievement in life. It would give me great pressure to show my gratitude to AuthorHouse Publishers for making this book possible. Special thanks to Editide editors for their propositions, remarks, understanding, and patience. They did a remarkable job. I am also grateful to the Faculty of the School of Public Policy and Administration at Walden University, especially my former dissertation mentor, Dr. Sally Thomason, and my former dissertation chair, Dr. David W. Hays, for their contributions to this book and the role they played in my KAM research project.

This book was inspired by the collapse of the stock market and the mortgage market failure in 2008 and the lessons future retirees and investors can learn from the U.S. banking-system failure in 1929 and the Great Depression.

PREFACE

This book is a version of Walden University's unit of study: the Breadth, Depth, and Application components of the advanced Knowledge Area Module (KAM) V. KAM V is one of the required research projects in the School of Management for students completing their PhD in Public Policy and Administration. The university uses this research project to train students to become expert in public management. Others' research contributions to this book appear in the literature review and studies cited in my dissertation research project.

Chapter 1, the Breadth component, explores the chronology of the Social Security program prior to the Great Depression and the events that led to the establishment of the Social Security program. The lessons that can be learned from the collapse of the stock market and the U.S. banking system failure in 1929 as they relate to the Great Depression are central to this chapter. Additionally, the success and deficiencies in the Social Security program are other important areas illustrated in Chapter 1. Also, in the Breadth component, I use a narrative-research format to examine other countries' social security systems, and provide some practical and theoretical examples of those countries' systems. Specifically, I describe how those countries' examples can be used to rectify deficiencies in the U.S. Social Security program and provide strategic plans to strengthen the program in the next 50 years.

In Chapter 2, the Depth Component, I use a comparative-analysis model to determine cost benefits of privatization of the U.S. Social Security system. I point to different studies to explore the contention that women, African Americans, low-income earners, and elders under the current system are likely to receive lower Social Security benefits after their retirement. Also, in Chapter 2, I examine studies showing that low-income workers, African Americans, and elders have almost no financial wealth at their retirement. The distribution of bequeathal wealth among minority retirees in the United States is highly unequal. This chapter includes an annotated bibliography and recommendations.

In Chapter 3, the Application Component, I investigate what led to deficiencies in the Social Security system. In another important part of this chapter, I explore the assertion that the Social Security program will be terminated within 20 years, if immediate steps are not taken by lawmakers to rectify the program's problems. In this chapter, I review literature to demonstrate that the privatization of Social Security or the alternative plans of privatization might be magic solutions to the deficiencies in the program. Also in Chapter 3, I illustrate alternative plans to privatization, such as the San Diego Supplemental Pension Savings Plan (SPSP), Galveston Alternative Plan (GAP), and NYC Deferred Compensation (457 plan), and the impact these plans would have on stabilization of the Social Security program.

Chapter 4 addresses the empirical research and the role of government in the Social Security system. The literature included describes political ideologies of social security in democratic nations globally, and how political parties view their social security systems as they try to stabilize their systems.

PART I

BREADTH COMPONENT

Napoleon Imarhiagbe, PhD

Introduction

Every human-being whether poor or rich, Black or White, must face the inevitable: old age. Most U.S. citizens are likely to apply for Social Security Insurance or retirement benefits during their lifetimes. Social Security is vital because most U.S. older workers will retire from their jobs when they have reached the age of 65 and be left with no visible alternative work opportunities. They are likely to depend on Social Security or retirement benefits for survival until their inevitable death (Schulz & Gorin, 2005).

The purpose of this book is to explore why the Social Security Insurance Policy was developed, and the impact it has on the citizens of the United States. Social Security policy was implemented in the United States to improve the lives of citizens over the age of 65, based on the nation's economic conditions in the mid-20th century (Myers, 1975). In a democratic society like the United States, legislators formulate public policy based on the social, economic, and security needs of the nation. Therefore, this book will rigorously examine what led to the development of Social Security insurance, partially in an attempt to determine whether it is necessary to reform the Social Security program. It will also look at the economic implications on elderly and retired workers if the Social Security program is reformed. In addition, it is very important to know whether the Social Security program will continue to meet the stated goals of providing an economic foundation for millions of Americans during this 21st century. Furthermore, the economic policy of the Great Depression and the foundation of the United States Social Security program are critically explored. Comparative analysis is used to examine other nations' social security systems and how different countries' programs work. Finally, this book will also consider the economic implications of the rise of the elderly population and how democratic governance affects the Social Security program.

Social Security has been classified as one of the most important government policies in U.S. history. One researcher, Ferrara (1980), considered the program to be the treasure of U.S. welfare. Some of the nation's most respected public policy analysts argued that the Social Security program was one of the most effective social and economic policies the United States government ever developed.

The program provides economic life support for millions of older U.S. citizens, and today continues to enjoy significant support from the public and policymakers. Sutton (2005) affirmed that "as an intergenerational compact arising out of the depths of the Great Depression, Social Security has been the cornerstone of

America's commitment to economic justice for the aged and infirm" (p. 45). In fact, it was a program implemented during the Great Depression about 80 years ago by policymakers to show that the U.S. government cares about the well-being of its citizens. Even critics of Social Security admit the program has contributed heavily to improvement in the lives of the elderly and poor in the United States (Ferrara, 1980). By any standard, the Social Security program is one of the most important and effective federal policies of the last century.

More to its credit, the program has helped root out poverty among older citizens at the peak of the Depression, and continues to be the backbone of their economic survival. Moreover, the level of poverty among the elderly has been reduced dramatically since the Social Security Act was enacted by Congress in 1935 (Ferrara, 1980). Indeed, since the Social Security program was established 8 decades ago, it continues to be the major source of income for the majority of retired workers. Nearly all workers contribute to the program through their payroll taxes, and they become eligible for their benefits after retirement (Sutton, 2005).

> In an insurance program, individuals are paid benefits after various contingencies occur. The amount of these benefits depend solely on how much the individual has paid into the program in the past, and the benefits are paid regardless of whether the individual really needs them. (Ferrara, 1980, p. 6)

Social Security is an insurance program that pays benefits to an individual when he or she retires, is disabled, dies, or is hospitalized. The way Social Security benefits are calculated grants higher benefit amounts to those individuals who have paid higher Social Security taxes. Generally, benefits are paid to an individual whether or not the person needs them (Ferrara, 1980).

Development of Social Security Around the World

Policymakers around the world share common concerns and have introduced social insurance programs to address poverty among elderly and poor citizens. A type of social security was implemented in the late 19th century in Europe. The program was first established in Germany in 1889, followed by Demark in 1891 (Pechman, Aaron, & Tausig, 1968). Today no country in Europe lacks a social security program. Pechman et al. (1968) found that 19 of the 23 nations of Central and South America, 24 of the 34 African countries, 8 of the 11 Middle and South East countries, 11 of the 24 nations in Asia, Oceania, and

North America, including Canada and the United States, have Social Security programs. Indeed, about 70 countries in the world have public programs that provide benefits for old age, disability, and survivors of deceased workers. Most of these 70 countries rely solely on social insurance programs. Some countries have universal pensions. In most countries' universal social security pension systems, benefits are tied to workers' earning histories. In some countries, social retirement (social insurance) systems were designed to make "an individual's earnings [supplemented] by a spousal benefit package (including survivor's benefits) for those who spent less carrier time in the paid labor force" (Stark, Folbre, & Shaw, 2005, p. 170). "Canada, Demark, Norway, Finland, and Sweden-maintain a universal pension plan to provide the basic benefits and use the insurance programs for supplementary pensions reflecting the individual's prior earnings" (Pechman et al., 1968, p. 274).

In most industrialized societies, a social insurance or social retirement plan is the major source of income for the aged. This program has been instrumental in reducing poverty among the poor and elders in these countries. Sweden and Germany's social insurance programs have the greatest success in reducing poverty among women and elders. In 2000, the poverty rate for the elderly in Sweden dropped almost 68%, whereas poverty declined for older women in Germany by 60% (Stark et al., 2005). The United States and United Kingdom also were able to reduce senior citizens' poverty by 36–39 percentage points in 1999 and 2000 (Stark et al., 2005). Canada's Guaranteed Income Supplement (GIS) system, established in 1929, has done a remarkable job of improving the lives of its citizens, better than most industrialized countries (but only slightly more than the United States). Canada has experienced a 45% poverty-rate reduction for all households, including older citizens. One reason is that about 90% of Canadian elders receive GIS benefits, compared to 60% of U.S. elders who are eligible for Social Security Income (SSI) benefits. In fact, Canada has been more successful than the United States because it spends public money differently, prioritizing its universal Old Age Security by joining it with the GIS. "This program has no asset test and a relatively simple annual application process, which permits an income test integrated with income tax filing so as to avoid stigma and encourage take-up" (Stark et al., 2005). Research by Stark et al. (2005) also revealed that:

> Canada allocates close to 9 percent of its total tax and transfer retirement income spending on GIS, while the United States allocates less than 2 percent of government retirement income spending on the SSI program. SSI benefits accrue to about 10 percent of the United States aged; GIS benefits reach 33 percent of Canadian elders. (p. 173)

In the United States, for workers to be eligible for Social Security benefits they must work at least 10 years: "Spouses and in some cases divorced spouses of retired workers are eligible for a dependent benefit of 50 percent of the retired worker's benefit, and surviving widows/ widowers are entitled to 100 percent of the deceased workers' benefit" (Stark et al., 2005, p. 184). Social insurance covers the unemployed, as well as all employed and self-employed persons in Israel, the United States, Japan, The Netherlands, Switzerland, and the United Kingdom. In the United States and about 20 other countries, practically all employed and self-employed persons are covered by social security programs, and some unemployed people are eligible for benefits. Whatever the extent of the benefits different countries offers their citizens, social security programs have been successful in reducing poverty among poor families and older people, especially in Sweden, Germany, Canada, and the United States, since the program was first introduced by in Germany in 1889 (Pechman et al., 1968).

Social Security Before the Great Depression

Prior to the implementation of the Social Security system, family farms dominated as the economic institution of the 19th century in the United States. Farming was the economic backbone for most families and the nation. The economy the government advocated was based on individual effort. Individuals' drive to provide for themselves and their families with the income they earned from farming supported them, with little or no government assistance. As individuals grew older, they reduced their farm work and allowed younger family members to take over the major share of the workload. Older citizens who could no longer work had to rely on financial assistance from their children or family members (Pechman et al., 1968). The income most families earned from farming was sufficient to support their families and their elderly parents. The economic conditions of U.S. families were ample and sufficient to address their basic needs. The money families spent to care for their elderly parents was less than they would have to spend today. Problems for the elderly emerged gradually, when the economy of the nation changed mostly from farming to industrial work during the second half of the 19th century. Industrial development led to the decline in the economic status of the aged. MaCurdy and Shoven (1999) demonstrated that "the increasing mechanization of production required vigorous and competitive workers. The aged who had held the reins of economic power in the agrarian economy were at a distinct disadvantage in the industrialization world" (p. 19). Indeed, industrial work was quite difficult for older citizens. As a result, most of them stopped working because of the harsh nature of the jobs. Research by Pechman et al. (1968) supported this position:

> As technical innovations and capital accumulation increased productivity and general living standards, it became more difficult for the older workers to share fully the fruits of progress. To the extent that he could not adapt to new techniques, his position in the labor market deteriorated, and his subsequent poverty stood out more sharply. (p. 30)

In fact, older workers were less useful in the new industrial economy. Consequently, their economic power and living standards diminished. Most who were unemployed relied on family members for support (Pechman et al., 1968). As industries transformed the nation's economy, they reduced children's support for their elderly parents, because most grown children were working longer hours at their factory jobs. This was the first time in the nation's history when more industries existed than farms. Indeed, industrialization changed U.S. families' lives because most people no longer needed their children to work on their farms to support their families. Pechman et al. (1968) demonstrated that "families in the city found children less advantageous than did families on the farms, and the size of families declined sharply" (p. 30). Aged parents became a burden to their children. In most cases, it was not possible for aged parents to accompany their children to their factory jobs, unlike farm jobs where they were able to work side-by-side with their children. Family ties weakened as a result of the arrival of the industrial economy. Fewer families had sufficient time to care for their elderly parents.

A new problem emerged not only for the elderly but also for the entire family, because the nation' economy collapsed. In 1929, the economic crash that brought on the Depression added more to the hardships of the poor and elderly (L. Merriam, 1946). Ferrara (1980) reinforced the position that the Great Depression clearly led to the increase in the problems of elders, and many children who had previously supported their parents were compelled to stop doing so because of the economic hardships of the Depression. The Depression eradicated workers' savings and deprived millions of workers of the ability to support themselves and their aged parents.

During the Great Depression, most families were unable to support their aged parents because younger adults were also unemployed. Most important, older workers could not get sufficient support from local governments because governments themselves were in deep economic recession. In addition, public assistance was unable to provide enough relief for the poor and elderly because of the high rate of poverty and the many people across the country who required assistance.

Public charities that provided support for poor people and senior citizens were insufficient to withstand the economic hardships of the Great Depression. This was the period when millions of Americans were unable to provide basic needs for their families. In addition, the collapse of the stock market had a devastating effect on the economy, increasing the already massive unemployment, which overwhelmed state and local governments. Under U.S. law and practice, states and local governments had the responsibility to provide assistance to those who were unemployed. Providing relief to those who were poor and elderly was not an easy task for most state governments. One reason was that many states had not modernized their tax systems to generate sufficient revenue to provide assistance to destitute citizens. Revenues generated from property taxes were insufficient. State and local governments were short of cash; they did not even have the resources and capacity to pay for the salaries of their employees (L. Merriam, 1946). Another problem was that many states were unable to raise funds or borrow money from banks to provide relief for their constituencies. L. Merriam's (1946) study revealed one of the hindrances preventing state and local governments from being able to borrow money from banks during the Great Depression was that

> relief was in the main an operating expense of government and not an outlay for capital improvements; and laws restricted borrowing for expense. Some state constitutions gave the state government no powers with respect to relief, prohibiting them from borrowing for an object over which they no power. (p. 11)

In addition, not only did state and local governments not have constitutional power over the currency but also they had no influence over the banking system.

The worst problem was that many states were in debt, which made it very difficult for them to borrow money from banks to meet the emergency needs of the people. Banks could not lend money to states and local governments because governments did not have enough revenue to pay back loans. Most states were already in default on their interest payments and had outstanding balances on their loans. Thus, they were unable to borrow additional funds from banks (L. Merriam, 1946).

Another reason local governments were unable to obtain loans was that most U.S. banks were in precarious shape, facing financial failure. Customers facing financial hardship and those who were unemployed were compelled to withdraw their money from banks. Adding to the banking market's woes was that "most investors would not take the bond and notes off the banker's hands" (L. Merriam, 1946, p.11). Indeed, the banking system was in a poor condition, and the nation's economy was in shambles. Most people who were laid off were unable to find new jobs. Most breadwinners were unable to support their elderly parents and their families. The problems of the Great Depression not only caused financial failure but also public disorder. The problems of the Great Depression brought a breakdown in law and order, including economic hardship and social change (L. Merriam, 1946). States and local governments had problems maintaining law and order and were frustrated by their inability to provide adequate assistance to those who were unemployed and poor. Under these circumstances, state and local governments were forced to turn to the federal government to get funds to provide relief for those people desperately in need of assistance.

The message was clear that most Americans needed support from the federal government. President Roosevelt was compelled to galvanize Congress to develop an economic policy to heal the suffering of the people. In fact, the Social Security program was a prescription for healing the pain of millions of people who were unemployed; especially the poor and elderly (Ferrara, 1980).

Analyzing Social Security Problems

Social Security is not a separate entity from the federal government (Dreher, 2005). Social Security payroll taxes paid by workers are part of the federal government's revenues and the U.S. government can decide to use the contributions made by workers into the Social Security trust fund to finance other programs (Garrett & Rhine, 2005). Workers have no legal right to say how their Social Security taxes should be used. Rounds (200) affirmed that Social Security is a form of welfare benefit. It is unlike the individual private accounts where workers have control over the money or contributions that have been invested (Rounds, 2000).

Rounds (2000) stressed that Social Security is not an insurance program. The courts also ruled in *Helvering v. Davis* (2002) that a worker's retirement benefit is dependent on a political decision. Policymakers have the right to make decisions about what to do with Social Security retirement benefits. Rounds claimed that policymakers have the power to change the rules of the Social Security program. According to Dreher (2005), policymakers have the legal right to reduce retirement benefits, increase the retirement age, raise payroll taxes, or offer alternative plans. Policymakers can even terminate Social Security retirement benefits (Dreher, 2005). *Helvering v. Davis* (2002) illustrated that Congress has the right to alter, amend, or repeal any provision of the Social Security Act. The Court ruled against a comparison of the Social Security program to insurance. The centerpiece of the court ruling was that workers have no legal right to Social Security benefits. Social Security was structured to allow the government to collect tax revenues through the Federal Insurance Contributions Act (FICA) and commingle them with general assets (Rounds, 2000). This means that Congress has the power to issue Social Security payments out of general assets to those who are eligible.

Social Security benefits are part of total federal outlays (Rounds, 2000). Program assets are not separated from other federal revenues (Dreher, 2005). The federal government can use the Social Security surplus to cover other expenses or deficits (Dreher, 2005). When other parts of the budget are in deficit, budget surpluses in Social Security automatically cover the gap (Rounds, 2000). If the revenues generated from Social Security taxes were only used by the Social Security Administration (SSA) to cover benefits for retirees or participants, the program would not be facing a budget deficit (Garrett & Rhine, 2005).

The Implications of the Burgeoning Elderly Population

The elderly population will continue to grow at a high rate in the United States, according to the Congressional Budget Office (2001). The number of people over the age of 65 is likely to increase more than 90% in the next 3 decades. The population was 36 million in 2001 and by 2030 will increase to 69 million. The number of adults under the age of 65 increased to 170 million in 2001 and was projected to increase to 195 million in 2030. The number of elderly people will continue to increase at a higher rate, whereas the nonelderly population is likely to rise at a slower rate, as life spans continue to lengthen. The adults under the age of 65 are expected to pay the taxes to continue to support their elders (Congressional Budget Office, 2001).

Experts projected that when the baby-boom generation retires, the federal government will be compelled to increase the amount and percentage of money spent on Social Security. Moreover, spending on Social Security is projected to increase by 50% over the next 3 decades, which will be 4.2% of the nation's total output (gross domestic product). Consequently, these changes are likely to pose a major challenge to the United States economy in the near future, unless Social Security problems are addressed within a short time (Congressional Budget Office, 2001).

The Sustainability of the U.S. Social Security System

The largest federal social program, Social Security, is facing a crisis. According to recent predictions, the Social Security program will not be able to generate enough revenue to meet all of its beneficiaries' needs by the end of 2042 (Svihula & Estes, 2008). If the existing law is not changed, the Social Security program will either have to scale back all of beneficiary payments or will have to depend on appropriate funding by Congress, from general tax revenues, to meet its planned responsibilities and obligations. As this program has become significant to a number of dependents, disabled, and retired U.S. citizens, any changes in the program will raise concerns for many people (Steuerle, Carasso, & Cohen, 2004).

For people older than 60 years, the Social Security program is a major component of their retirement income, and most have been receiving the benefits since the age of 62 (Kastner & Rector, 2005). In fact, the Social Security payments received by most people constitute the majority of their retirement income (SSA, 2003); for more than 64% of retirees, payments constitute more than 50% of their income. A majority of people in the United States who are not receiving their Social Security income yet expect that the benefits they will be receiving will comprise most of their income. The average person has saved around $20,000 as part of a retirement plan. People who approached retirement in 2004 had only $60,000 set aside in Individual Retirement Accounts (IRAs) and 401 (k) accounts, which equates to only $400 per month, as part of their retirement income (Svihula & Estes, 2008). Social Security provides more than 40% of preretirement income for the average retiree (Acomb, 2005). Social Security programs are barely adequate to keep recipients out of poverty, and many employees in their 40s and 50s have a weak financial future (Svihula & Estes, 2008). Typically, people are not able to start saving early and sometimes are not able to save enough to put aside an adequate amount for retirement. Thus, they are forced to depend on the Social Security program.

Social Security must be capable of providing benefits at a level that allows all people in the United States to stay out of poverty. Workers who are paying into this system and workers who are eligible for receiving benefits must align

(Acomb, 2005). Workers must understand the notion of paying into the system to receive benefits. If the program fails to maintain this responsibility, it may create the perception that beneficiaries depend on the state (Steuerle et al., 2004). Removing this interconnection between those who pay into the system and those who receive benefits will lead to confusing Social Security with an insurance program. In traditional insurance programs, a person pays into the system, voluntarily or involuntarily, gaining the right to future benefits. A way must be found to preserve the Social Security program as it was intended to be in the face of demographic trends that contribute to the erosion of its financial structure.

Social Security: An Evolutionary Process

Social Security must adapt to a changing economic and social institutional environment if the program is to continue to be successful. The history of Social Security is like an evolutionary process: program changes are based on the economic conditions of the time. Based on this notion, a program that is suitable for today's economy may not be suitable for tomorrow's economy (Munnell, 1977). Robertson (1985) supported the notion that when the Social Security Act was passed about 81 years ago, the nation had been in a serious economic depression for almost 6 years. The social and economic condition the nation experienced at that time included the following:

1. More workers than jobs and a consequently high unemployment rate,
2. A small elderly population relative to the younger potential working population,
3. Relatively undeveloped reliable institutions through which an individual could invest and save for future, and
4. An almost completely undeveloped system of private pensions and other employee benefits provided by employers (Robertson, 1985, p. 41).

Undoubtedly, the social and economic conditions of today are quite different from those when the Social Security program was implemented. Presently, more jobs exist than when the program was established 80 years ago. The size of the elderly population has doubled, and more people are receiving Social Security benefits than before. In addition, workers have greater investment opportunities and more people have access to private pensions.

Since Social Security was developed, the structure of the program has not changed. Some experts argue that the program is becoming too large and outdated. Social

Security was established in the heart of the Great Depression, and many of its features were structured to fit the economic and social circumstances of those times: "Many economic and social impacts that might have been thought desirable then are no longer desirable now" (Ferrara, 1980, p. 4). The Great Depression is gone; it is time to reform the system.

Benefits Paid by Social Security

The Social Security law was passed by Congress in 1935. The original Social Security Act established four programs. Two were social insurance programs: old-age insurance, and unemployment insurance. Another was public assistance for needy elders, needy dependent children, and the needy blind. The fourth program provided welfare services for maternal and child health, crippled children, child welfare, vocational rehabilitation, and public health work. Survivors insurance was added to the program in 1939, and disability insurance in 1956. Health insurance (Medicare) began in 1965 (Chen, 1980). Payroll taxes for old age benefits commenced on January 1, 1937. The first monthly Social Security benefits were issued to those who were eligible for them in 1940. The Social Security program serves more than 90% of the working population (Munnell, 1977). Between 1966 and 1976, the Social Security program paid $80 billion in benefits for eligible applicants and recipients. The program pays more than $83 billion annually in benefits to those who are retired, disabled, dependent, and survivors. Working and retired people would be paid more than $4 trillion in the future (Munnell, 1977). Over 95% of retired workers and senior citizens in 1998 were receiving Social Security benefits, and the number was likely to increase in the near future (Baker & Weisbrot, 1999). Similarly, in 2001, more than 45 million retired workers, their families, and survivors received Social Security benefits payments (Congressional Budget Office, 2001). Data from the SSA shows the number of people who received Social Security payments, average monthly benefits, and payroll taxes (see Table 1).

Table 1

Social Security Beneficiaries

Numbers of Social Security beneficences	$
Retired workers	28.5 million
Disabled workers	5.0 million
Spouses of deceased workers	5.1 million
Spouses of retired or disabled workers	3.0 million
Children of retired, disabled or deceased workers	3.8 million
Total number of beneficiaries	45.4 million
Average Monthly Social Security Benefits	
Retired workers	$845
Disabled workers	$787
Spouses of deceased workers	$790
Spouses of retired or disabled worker	$417
Children of retired, disabled or deceased workers	$406
Workers	
Numbers of workers in employment covered by Social Security	152 million
Social Security Payroll Tax	
Tax rate (paid half by employer and half by employee)	12.4%
Limit on worker's annual earnings subject to the tax	$80, 400
Maximum tax owed (paid half by employer and half by employee	$9,970

Note. From *Social Security: A Primer,* by Congressional Budget Office, 2001, retrieved from http://www.cbo.gov/ftpdocs/32xx/doc3213/EntireReportpdf

The Growth of the Social Security Benefits and Taxes

Social Security is the largest of all government programs. It constitutes one-fourth of the federal budget. The program payments were estimated to cost the federal government $430 billion in 2002, roughly one-quarter of the entire federal budget (Congressional Budget Office, 2001). The government spending on welfare, together with Social Security, accounted for nearly half of federal spending, excluding interest payments on the federal debt. In the past 2 decades, Social Security benefits have grown tremendously. The government was compelled to raise taxes several times to continue to finance the increase in benefits. In 1977, Congress implemented a massive tax increase policy to prevent the Social Security program from bankruptcy. This was one of the largest tax increases in the nation's history. Under the tax law, the payroll tax increased steadily through 1990.

> In 1965, employers and employees paid a combined tax of 7.25 percent on the first $4,800 of wages; by 1975, the combined tax had increased to 11.7 percent of the first $14,100. By 1977, the maximum taxable wage had increased to $16,500. In the twelve-year period the maximum tax levied on a covered worker has climbed from $348 to $1,930, more than a fivefold increase. (Munnell, 1977, p. 1)

To continue to keep the program active, the federal government needs a higher rate of Social Security tax (Munnell, 1977). One way to fund the Social Security program over a 75-years period is to increase the payroll tax by 2.19%.

In contrast, MaCurdy and Shoven (1999) argued that it is unnecessary to increase payroll taxes if the federal government can cut workers' retirement benefits. They supported the notion of a 15% cut in recipient benefits across the board: "That is not only a 15 percent cut in benefits for somebody who is retiring next month or next decade; that is a 15 percent cut for everyone getting benefits today" (p. 2). For example, someone who is receiving $800 monthly benefit would be reduced to $680. A widow's or survivor's monthly benefits would be reduced from $600 to $500. MaCurdy and Shoven affirmed that if the federal government waits until the trust fund is exhausted in 2030, to fix the program's problem, the benefit would be reduced by 25% and recipients' benefits would drop from $800 to $600 while the widow benefit would be reduced from $600 to $450.

Walker (2003) supported the notion that the federal government should reduce the benefits of future retiree workers to balance Social Security accounts. Younger workers would properly have more benefit reduction than older people. For example, people born in 1955 are unlikely to experience benefit reductions until they reached the age of 83, "while those born in 1985 would receive lower benefits than under either [Government Accounting Office's] benefit reduction or tax increase benchmarks in all years of retirement. Consequently, lifetime benefits would be reduced more for younger generations" (Walker, 2003, p. 21).

Another way to reform the U.S. Social Security program is by copying from the Australian and Sweden systems: "Australia has moved to a system of private mandatory individual accounts as its form of retirement saving and the system has been widely supported by both organized labor and employers" (MaCurdy & Shoven, 1999, p. 10). Australian social security works like the 401(k) system, and workers accounts are operated through businesses and unions. The Swedish government has introduced a similar method for its workforce. In this system, workers are allowed to redirect 2.5% of their covered payroll to accounts managed by financial brokers (MaCurdy & Shoven, 1999).

Walker (2003) supported the idea that the federal government should reduce defense spending to accommodate the growth in the Social Security program. However, this may not materialize because of the ongoing war in Iraq. It can be assumed that defense spending and the Homeland Security budget will continue to grow, as the government professes to protect the nation from terrorists. Another idea is that the government can raise more funds for the Social Security program if the retirement age limit increases. For example, the retirement age can be increased from 62 to 71(Shaw & Mysiewicz, 2006). Using this idea would prevent the government from raising Social Security payroll taxes, which is largely opposed by the public. Without a doubt, people oppose the notion of increasing the retirement age because they believe they may not have enough time to enjoy their retirement benefits before they die (Saving, 2006). However, fixing the Social Security program's problems now is advisable, because if adjustment is not made to the program, according to the Congressional Budget Office (2001), by 2030 the Social Security will take about two-thirds of the federal budget.

Argument for the Reform of the Social Security Program

The Social Security program, without a doubt, is one of the most effective federal economic programs implemented in the United States in the mid-20th century. The program is one of the least controversial policies developed to improve the lives of citizens over the age of 65. The majority of U.S. citizens have continued to support the program since it was established 82 years ago (Munnell, 1977). But recently, Social Security has received some negative reviews from some experts who contend the program is costing the country billions of dollars annually, and that it has a negative impact on the economy. Some studies showed that future young taxpayers may not receive a fair return on the taxes they pay for Social Security programs. In 1998, former U.S. President Bill Clinton elucidated some of the most important issues confronting the Social Security program:

> The fiscal crisis in Social Security affects every generation. ... If we wait too long to fix it, the burden on society of taking care of our [baby boom] generation's Social Security obligations will lower your income and lower your ability to take care of your children to a degree most of

us who are parents think would be horribly wrong and unfair to you and unfair to the future prospects of the United States. ... And if nothing is done by 2029, there will be a deficit in the Social Security trust fund, which will either require—if you just wait until then—a huge tax increase in the payroll tax, or just about a 25 percent in Social Security benefits. (as cited in MaCurdy & Shoven, 1999, p. 3)

President Clinton laid out why it is important to reform the Social Security program in a short period. Policymakers should not continue to procrastinate to resolve the problems that engulf the Social Security program, nor should they leave these problems to be solved by coming generations. They must not wait until the program is insolvent before finding solutions to it, because it will be more expensive and time consuming to fix the problems later (Saving, 2006). Taking action to solve Social Security problems "would not only promote increased budgetary flexibility in the future and stronger economic growth but would also make less dramatic action necessary than if we wait" (Walker, 2003, p. 14).

Actions taken today to prevent Social Security from bankruptcy will give the government a significant advantage in planning for future retirees. Indeed, the collapse of the Social Security program is foreseeable and policymakers cannot continue to ignore the trend. Rather, they must make sure to buoy the current system. Politically, and by law, it is the duty of policymakers to reform Social Security, because they were its architects. Indeed, change in any government program must be enacted by lawmakers, and must pass through the political channel.

Social Security Reform and Democratic Governance

The Social Security program was established through the political system, and often changed or reformed through the democratic process. Any product or instrument for the public is quite difficult to change without the majority of the public and elected officials' support. The Social Security program is unlike an individual private property that a person has a right to change. Social Security is a bureaucratic institution and the program is operating through a political process (Ferrara, 1980). It is not a private institution operating through a market process. Those who administer the program have no authority to change the program in a way that would be better for taxpayers and beneficiaries.

Under democratic governance, political parties must adhere to one process: They must debate whether any justifications exist to reform the Social Security program. In some cases, proponents and opponents present their experts in Congress to defend or attack the idea of reforming the Social Security program. Undoubtedly, changing or reforming the Social Security system is a tedious process, in part because any reform of the program must be debated by different interest groups. Advocates for the reform of Social Security must be able to convince the general public and political leaders to support their ideas for reform. For interest groups and taxpayers to get their wishes, they must go through political channels (Ferrara, 1980). Those who wish to reform the Social Security program should start a national political movement to gather enough votes to support their ideas for reform of the program.

Indeed, Social Security would be difficult to change because the majority of the people involved are political novices and do not understand how the program works. Moreover, they do not understand the economic implications of reform of the Social Security system. Most people do not know that the program is facing difficult problems, and that the program may become bankrupt in the future (Ferrara 1980).

Another important reason the Social Security program is very difficult to reform is that there is one set of benefit provisions for everyone: One very particular system is imposed on all participants. Ferrara (1980) also reinforced the contention that the Social Security program is operated on a pay-as-you-go system, and individuals are not paying for their own benefits. The way Social Security was designed, "individuals are forced to save for their retirement through Social Security instead of saving on their own, and the money paid into the program [is not] saved but [immediately] paid out to current recipients" (Ferrara, 1980, p. 26). Reform of Social Security is quite significant because reform will enable the government to balance the current program's account. It will also bring the program up to standards. The government will gain the opportunity to create different programs that offer alternative retirement plans, which may be better than the one the current system offers. In addition, the government will be able to resolve the problems in the current program.

Other Nations' Social Security Reform Models

A few researchers (Burgoon, Demetriades, & Underhill, 2008; Kay & Kritzer, 2001; Korczyk, 2005; Matijascic & Kay, 2006; Mesa-Lago, 2007) compared the

U.S. Social Security retirement system with other nations' retirement plans. In the last quarter of the 20th century, the most radical transformation of social policy reform took place in Latin America. The trend to reform retirement plans began in Chile in 1981 and spread to other Latin American countries (Kay & Kritzer, 2001). The Chilean retirement reform model started at a time when the country's retirement system was facing a serious financial crisis. Prior to the reform of the Chilean PAYGO system in 1981, the program was badly mismanaged. Chile's retirement program had low coverage and high administrative fees. In addition, the program was unable to sustain higher retirement benefits promised to workers (Borzutzky, 2005). The reform became a model for many countries in the region, when most people thought that Chile's retirement system would be "impossible to solve within the prevailing paradigm" (Mesa-Lago, 2007, p. 185).

In Latin America, countries established three types of structural reform: private, parallel, and mixed-models. Bolivia, Chile, the Dominican Republican, El Salvador, Mexico, and Nicaragua terminated their public retirement programs and replaced them with private systems. Colombia and Peru have a parallel retirement system. Their public systems were not dismantled, but governments introduced retirement programs that allowed the public to compete with private systems. Argentina, Costa Rica, and Ecuador's reform systems are mixed: "The public systems continue as the first pillar of an integrated scheme while a private system became the second pillar and pays supplementary pensions" (Mesa-Lago, 2007, p. 182). Other countries in the region, such as Cuba, Guatemala, Haiti, Honduras, Panama, Paraguay, and Venezuela have not reformed their public retirement systems. However, some may soon follow the footsteps of their neighbors by reforming their retirement systems (Mesa-Lago, 2007).

The significance of the public retirement reform in Latin America and other countries in this research is that it will enable comparative analyses of reform systems and will enable researchers to measure the extent of the success of the retirement plan reform in Chile and other countries (Ball, 2005). More importantly, it will enable stakeholders to choose the best alternative, which may be instrumental for U.S. Social Security reform. Matijascic and Kay (2006) reinforced the notion that social security reform, specifically in Chile, should be reexamined. They contended that the personal individual account system introduced in Chile and other countries should be thoroughly evaluated to know the extent of the success of the new reform: "Individual pension savings accounts in Latin America promised to improve compliance and raise benefits in a cost-effective manner, while at the same time raising savings rates, which in turn promote economic growth" (p. 1).

In 2002, the European Council met in Gothenburg, Sweden, to discuss how to reform the nation's retirement system. Most European Union (EU) member states still operate PAYGO retirement systems, similar to the U.S. system. Experts agreed that retirement system reform in Western Europe and the United States is inevitable (Shipman, 2003). In the PAYGO system, the government charges current workers to pay for future retired benefits. The PAYGO system is a simple transfer from workers to retirees (Shipman, 1995). The PAYGO system has no investment facet. Taxes paid by current workers are not invested or saved by the government to pay retirement benefits. Current workers rely on future generation to pay taxes for their benefits (Shipman, 2003). Experts agree that the PAYGO system is sustainable in the long run, if there is almost full employment, or the country has a large number of workers and a small number of retirees. However, in EU countries, apart from Ireland, the ratios of workers to retirees have fallen dramatically. In 2003, the ratio of workers in Austria and Belgium diminished by 2.1%. Shipman's study (2003) found that by 2025, most countries in the EU will not have enough workers to pay taxes sufficient to pay benefits for their retirees. For example, Germany will have more retirees than workers, with a ratio less than 1.1 to 1. As a result, most EU countries will not be able to maintain their PAYGO system in the long run.

Gran (2008) reinforced the position that the U.S. retirement system is in the same predicament as that of EU countries. Shipman (2003) suggested that both the United States and EU countries should move away from the PAYGO system, enabling them to continue to provide sustainable retirement benefits to their citizens. The United States and EU should operate a private investment-based retirement system (Gran, 2008). Shipman (2003) affirmed that private investment can not only help ensure the financial sustainability of pension systems but also can contribute to raising employee saving rates, thereby promoting a more dynamic economy with greater resources available for all citizens. This system would enable the United States and the EU to meet workers' retirement goals with a sustainable investment system.

In 1994, the World Bank encouraged countries to implement a private retirement system similar to the one implemented by Chile's government (Midgley & Tang, 2002). The World Bank sees the private retirement investment system as a way to stimulate economic growth (Midgley & Tang, 2002). Martin Feldstein, a notable professor at Harvard University, projected that the value of future benefits to the United States after privatizing Social Security would be $10–$20 trillion (as cited in Ferrara, 1997). G. S. Becker (1983), a Noble Prize winner in economics and A. Herberger, President of the American Economic Association, recommended the privatization of U.S. Social Security. One important part of the private systems is that those who withdraw from the public system will no longer pay taxes into the public retirement program; instead, those taxes would be used to pay into the private system (as cite din Gran, 2008). For example, in Chile's reform system, Chilean workers who choose the private system are not required to pay taxes in the old government-run retirement plan. They are allowed to keep all their money and invest in the private system (Ball, 2005). The government is the regulator of the system. The government is also the financial guarantor of last resort (Ball, 2005). Disney, Emmerson, and Wakefield (2008) found that in the British reform model, workers who chose private individual accounts must pay only part of their income in taxes to invest in the private system. Citizens must pay some part of the payroll taxes to help finance the continuation of benefits of the old system. Social Security experts have suggested that workers should be allowed to pay taxes into the old system to attract enough workers to choose the private system. Those who do not choose the private system, however, should be obliged to continue to pay taxes into the old system (Disney et al., 2008). Those workers who choose the private system and have paid into the old system for a certain number of years should be given a rebate after they retire, to compensate them for those payments (Disney et al., 2008).

In the Chilean reform model, when workers choose the new system, the government calculates the proportion of lifetime taxes the workers and their employees have already paid (Ball, 2005). This accounting enables the government to pay them a full refund for the past taxes they paid into the traditional retirement plan. Social Security reform would be one of the most important U.S. policy issues in this century if implemented. Most studies of Social Security reform suggest that the federal government should prefund benefits by integrating personal retirement accounts into the current system (Biggs, 2009; David, 2005; Gran; 2008; Queisser & Whitehouse, 2006; Updegrave, 2005). Two researchers (Kosterlitz, 2006; Updegrave, 2005) found that a personal account is a system that would allow younger workers to invest some of their Social Security taxes in stocks and bonds. This system would give younger workers the opportunity to earn a higher rate of return on their investments than they would accrue in Social Security benefits.

The Texas A&M Research Foundation data revealed that workers who are allowed to invest part of their FICA tax into a private account would still have an average of 6.2% return on their investment, even when the market is down: "workers that retired during a sluggish market year, the compounded value of all the gains will more than offset the losses" (as cited in Moore, 2003, p. 2). For the past 35 years, the stock market has outperformed what Social Security will pay in return for worker's payroll taxes, even when the market declined (Moore, 2003). However, personal investment accounts may be too risky for the federal government to undertake because of the recent collapse of the stock market (Schulz & Gorin, 2005). Researchers have yet to determine the full extent of the collapse of the stock market and the damage to personal retirement accounts.

Social Security Risks versus Private Investment Risks

Despite experts' concern about the fall of the stock market, Dwyer's study (2005) supported the use of private investment accounts by workers, especially those far from retirement. It is not financially risky for a young person just entering the workforce to try the private retirement system because he or she would not be retiring soon (Reno, 2005). A few bad years in the stock market is likely to be followed by other good years (Dwyer, 2005). Dwyer stressed that for a person close to retirement, because the period is shorter for his or her future earnings, a private retirement account is not good because a large decrease in stock market prices might wipe out retirement savings (Newberry, 2002). Weller (2005) reinforced the notion that a market risk would create problems for private retirement investors if the market stayed low for a long period. Campbell and Mungan (2007) affirmed that it is very difficult for experts to predict market failure. Market uncertainty is a major concern to every account holder or investor.

The risk in private retirement accounts can be prevented through a guarantee insurance program. Guaranteed insurance protection is necessary for private investment retirement accounts because they are a "protective shield against the considerable financial risks posed by market volatility and longevity" (p. 38). If the stocks go down, employees' retirement investments will not decline because their investments are protected by guaranteed insurance (Campbell & Mungan, 2007). The insurance guarantee allows workers to pay annual insurance fees to protect their assets or investments from a market decline. Campbell and Mungan stressed that workers purchasing insurance for their retirement savings investment is like buying insurance to protect a house in case of fire or disaster. Weller (2006) asserted that a private retirement investment account would be good for workers if there is no market risk. Dwyer (2005) contended that workers can minimize risk by investing in risk-free stocks. U.S. Treasury bills are risk free because people holding them to maturity will get the promised payment of dollars (Dwyer, 2005). Campbell and Mungan (2007) demonstrated that U.S. Treasury bills are obligations of the federal government. Treasury bills are short-term government securities, whereas corporate bonds are long-term securities. Corporate bonds are obligations of companies and they have higher risks because companies may not make the promised payments to bondholders. Risk is associated with the rate of return (Campbell & Mungan, 2007). Workers investing in U.S. Treasury bills are unlikely to get higher returns on their investments because Treasury bills have lower risk with a lower rate of return. President George W. Bush reinforced this notion in 2005 by stating that workers would be able to receive higher returns by investing in stocks and bonds rather than Treasury bills (as cited in Claude, 2005).

Dwyer (2005) found that corporate bonds and stocks carry higher risk but have a higher rate of return. The average rate of return per year, between 1955 and 2004, of financial assets for Treasury bills was 5.28 %, corporate bonds 6.80 %, and international stocks 20.70% (Dwyer, 2005). "A dollar invested in Treasury bills without any money taken out for 50 years becomes $12.71 in 2004. That same dollar invested in stock becomes $134.62, more than ten times more" (Dwyer, 2005, p. 7). Indeed, risk aligns with how much workers would make by investing in stocks or Treasury bills. A higher risk investment would generate a higher rate of return, and a lower risk investment would yield a lower rate of return for workers. Garrett and Rhine (2005) asserted Social Security has risks like the private retirement account system. The size of the Social Security program was estimated to be $1.4 trillion in 2003 (Garrett & Rhine, 2005). Garrett and Rhine's study revealed that since the enactment of Social Security in 1935, the program revenues have been greater than expenditures. According to Dwyer (2005), Social Security program payroll taxes have increased to $544 billion, while benefit payments rose to $406 billion in 2003. This resulted in a surplus of $138 billion in 2003. The program surplus was $156 billion in 2004, and will be exhausted in 2041.

Sixty years ago, there were 16.5 workers paying Social Security taxes for one retired worker receiving benefits. In 2005, there were 3.3 workers paying Social Security taxes for every retiree. This number will decrease to 2.17 workers in 2030 (Garrett & Rhine, 2005). Garrett and Rhine found that Social Security is in danger of failure because the number of workers paying FICA taxes has decreased in the past decades. The number will continue to decline due to the higher unemployment rate. In addition, there were 35 million retired workers in 2006. The number of retired workers receiving Social Security payments will increased by 35 million in 2030 (Garrett & Rhine, 2005).

President Bush declared in 2005 that the federal government will generate $200 billion to support Social Security in the year 2027. The program's annual deficits will grow more than $300 billion by 2033 (as cited in Burrell, 2004). Without the financial support of the government, the program will be exhausted and bankrupt (Burrell, 2004). Dreher (2005) contented that the government cannot support Social Security with $200 billion without increasing the national debt. He stressed that the federal government is already in debt. In 2005 the federal government debt was estimated to be $7.6 trillion. The debt rose to $11 trillion in 2008 (Dreher, 2005). It is expected to increase because of President Bush's 2008 $700 billion bailout of the financial market (Dreher, 2005). Dreher argued that Social Security's financial risks are very high. Garrett and Rhine (2005) commented that the program cannot continue to meet its payment obligations to retirees in the near future without the financial support of the federal government. In addition, the number of retirees is likely to increase more than workers paying Social Security taxes.

In the review of the literature, those who opposed a private investment account argued that it did not address the impact of Social Security bankruptcy on workers' retirement benefits and the national debt (Dattalo, 2007; Kennelly, 2005). Bryant (2005) reinforced the notion that Social Security has encountered financial problems before. This was in 1982, when the program trust fund was compelled to borrow $600 million to pay mandated benefits to workers on time (Bryant, 2005). In addition, the federal government will be forced to bail out Social Security to prevent the program from bankruptcy. As a result, it will increase the national debt.

Social Security is vital to the survival of current and future retired workers. The success of Social Security has made many experts refer to the program as the backbone of the nation's retired workers. Without a doubt, the Social Security program has been critical to the financial well-being of millions of U.S. citizens. In addition, the program has been effective in reducing poverty among elders and poor people (Sutton, 2005). Despite the success of Social Security, several studies (Ferrara, 1980; MaCurdy & Shoven, 1999; Walker, 2003) have shown that the program is underfunded, and future retirees may not be able to receive their benefits. Tanner (2002) also supported the notion that Social Security is facing bankruptcy. Tanner added that the program "faces irresistible demographic fiscal pressures that threaten the future retirement security of today's young workers" (p. 7). In addition, the Social Security system accumulation would be exhausted after the baby boomer generation starts retiring.

To generate more revenues for the program, some experts suggested the federal government should increase workers' payroll taxes 18–25% (Walker, 2003). Bosworth and Burtless (2000) reinforced the contention that the government is compelled to increase Social Security payroll taxes whenever the trust fund falls dangerously low. Taxes should continue to be increased until the trust fund is stabilized 100% of annual outlays. The increase in payroll tax should be modified periodically to keep Social Security a pay-as-you-go program with a reserve fund equal to 100% of the previous year's outlays.

Even though the Social Security program is underfunded, the government has been borrowing Social Security money to fund other programs. The problem is that the government has no plan to replace the money that has been borrowed from Social Security to fund other programs. Several researchers (Ferrara 1980; Meyer, 1987; D. S. Sanders, 1973; Shaw & Mysiewicz, 2006; Tucker, 2002; Walker, 2003) believed that it is unnecessary to increase workers' payroll taxes to resolve the problems facing Social Security program. Various options would strengthen Social Security. Some of them include the partial privatization of the program; a reduction in the retirement income of workers; an increase in taxes of higher income earners by 5 to 6% for 10 years (people earning $100-up); and allowing employees to invest some parts of their payroll income in stock markets. Another alternative is to automatically deduct 5% from every employee's weekly/biweekly income, which would be saved in a Direct Savings Account/Compte Epargne Direct (CED) account until he or she retires. Individuals will be able to accumulate interest in their accounts as the years go by. This money will eventually be given back to the individual on the first month he or she retires. As a result, most workers would be financially secure at the time they retire. Undoubtedly, one of these ideas may be suitable in rectifying Social Security' problems, if it is considered by policymakers.

Whatever the case, policymakers should carefully review all reform proposals and ensure that the chosen method reflects U.S. values of fairness. Indeed, the method must benefit all U.S. citizens, no matter their race or class. Policymakers must pay attention to the problems of Social Security and ensure that future generations continue to receive social insurance benefits.

Policymakers should think about the problems confronting future generations in our aging society. Reform of Social Security is necessary so that future generations do not inherit some of the economic problems facing us today:

Relieving them of some of the burden of today's financing commitments would help fulfill this generation's stewardship responsibility to future generations. It would also preserve some capacity for them to make their own choices by strengthening both budget and the economy they inherit. (Walker, 2003, p. 23)

Policymakers must act to address the problem as soon as possible. If not, the problems may cause economic hardship for future generations and may require more expensive solutions to resolve them. Social Security's problems are for this generation to resolve.

Conclusion

Social Security cannot have financial stability in the long run without restructuring the program (F. W. Becker, 2007; Garrett & Rhine, 2005; O'Neil, 2002; Shipman, 2003; Tanner, 2002). One proposal to reform Social Security is to increase the payroll tax by 2.2% (Howe & Jackson, 1998). However, Howe and Jackson (1998) pointed out that the percent tax increase would not be sufficient to fix Social Security's financial problems. The 2.2% tax increase would be equivalent to a 10% increase in every worker's personal income taxes. If the tax hike is implemented, Howe and Jackson warned it would cost the government almost $75 billion in 1 fiscal year.

Howe and Jackson (1998) stated that the additional 2.2% tax solution should not be permanent. An additional tax increase would be required by the government every year to keep the trust funds in balance over 75 years. The authors also asserted that the 2.2% solution is mainly based on the program's solvency. Although cutting benefits or increasing taxes may help balance the Social Security trust fund, it does not address other major problems, such as the declining rate of return for young workers. Social Security experts have not addressed the problem of the demographic change (Kennelly, 2005; Weller, 2007). Baby boomers face different retirement challenges than previous generations. In fact, they face two different retirement landscapes (Mayer, 2009): baby boomers are likely to spend more time not working than their parents and the retirement income of the baby boomer generation has decreased in comparison to that of their parents (Mayer, 2009).

The good news for boomers is that they enjoy better healthcare services than their parents. Baby boomers' life expectancies have increased significantly in the past decades (Mayer, 2009). Mayer (2009) demonstrated that an 85% chance that one member of a 65-year-old baby-boomer couple will live beyond the age of 85. There is also a 46% chance that one member of a baby boomer household will live past the age of 95. The bad news for the baby boomers is that they will need more retirement income because of their longer life expectancies. As a consequence, traditional Social Security retirement benefits may not be enough for baby boomer retirees (Mayer, 2009). Retirees' greater risk is that they are outliving their retirement savings. Most retirees, whether they are baby boomers or not, want sustainable retirement income (Butrica, Iams, & Smith, 2004). Social Security only replaces 40% of the average worker's preretirement earnings. Workers need about 70% of their preretirement wages to live comfortably after retirement (as cited in Biggs & Springstead, 2008). According to Weller (2007) a replacement ratio of 80% is adequate for retirement savings.

Moreover, the baby-boom generation and its increased life expectancy will force the SSA into paying more retirement benefits (Stark eta l., 2005). Stark et al. demonstrated that the current PAYGO design is structurally unproductive. Social Security will only be able to pay young workers about 0.58 % (for high-wage earners) and 2.93% (for low-wage workers) in the future (Siems, 2001). Barabas (2006) reinforced the notion that Social Security should change from PAYGO to a system based on savings and investment in private capital markets. A system based on individually owned and privately invested accounts is likely to yield more benefits to workers than benefits offered by SSA (Barabas, 2006; Garrett & Rhine 2005).

The benefits workers receive from private investment accounts are higher than those offered by the traditional PAYGO system. The average rate of return from the SSA for a couple born in 1973 is approximately 2.1%. The rate of return is likely to drop to between 1.7 and 1.9% if the federal government raises taxes or reduces benefits to keep the system in balance (Ferrara, 1999). Ferrara found that in a social security system that is privatized and fully funded, the money paid by a worker should be invested in real capital systems in the market. These investments will benefit the economy and create output and income. This production should finance a rate of return paid on such investments. Then, finally, this rate of return can finance higher retirement benefits for workers. Ferrara (1999) posited that PAYGO is not an investment system. It does not yield interest or a higher return on investment. Shipman (2003) demonstrated that PAYGO is simply a stable system that pays workers, based on their earning. Other nations, such as the United Kingdom, Chile, Brazil, Sweden, and Poland have implemented personal-investment accounts as a way to increase returns and benefits for their workers (F. W. Becker, 2007; Svihula & Estes, 2008).

Researchers reinforced the idea that reform of the Social Security program should be based on individual personal-investment accounts (Barabas, 2006; Biggs, 2003; Garrett & Rhine, 2005; Saving, 2006; Sutton, 2005; Tanner, 2002; Turner, 2005). Personal-investment accounts have been supported by Social Security experts. Despite the gain in support of personal accounts, policymakers have yet to unite behind the proposal to implement the plan, signifying a need to conduct more research to know whether the proposed investment plan will be effective in restructuring the Social Security program (Biggs, 2003; Garrett & Rhine 2005). Indeed, additional studies will confirm whether individual personal-investment accounts may be the best alternative to Social Security.

Another study found that the federal government would be compelled to raise taxes or cut benefits because over the past 48 years the non-Social Security part of the budget has had a deficit, except 1999 and 2000 (Ostaszewski, 1997). If the Social Security taxes fall short of Social Security benefit payments, the federal government must add funds to meet its payment obligation to retired workers. Ostaszewski (1997) revealed that most workers and the public at large would resist this notion of cutting benefits or increasing payroll taxes to continue to maintain the Social Security program. According to Frenzel, a Social Security expert at the Brookings Institution, "if you say you might have to raise payroll taxes, the no-tax crowd jumps all over you. Say you might have to decrease benefits, and the AARP and the Democrats will kill you" (as cited in Rohter, 2008, p. 20A). As a consequence, the federal government must provide alternative ways to solve the problems facing the Social Security retirement system. One suggestion is that the government should invest the Social Security trust fund in private capital markets. However, Ostaszewski affirmed that allowing the government to invest the Social Security trust fund in a private capital market would be socialization of a large portion of the U.S. economy. This would put much of the ownership into the hands of the U.S. government. Ostaszewski emphasized that it would be unfair for the government to invest the Social Security trust fund in private markets. This is because the plan will enable the federal government to become the nation's largest shareholder.

The federal government would have the power to control interest in nearly every U.S. company. Ostaszewski (1997) argued that it would be a cost-effective system if workers were allowed to invest their own retirement money through true privatization. A private system would allow workers to benefit from higher market returns without the risk of government investment in the economy. When the government invests, there is a higher possibility that political pressure will influence investment practices. Lawmakers may not use the profit made from the investment to provide service for those workers who pay Social Security payroll taxes. It is unlike the individual private accounts where workers have full ownership over their investments (Kosterlitz, 2006; Walter, 2010).

Some of the literature reviewed addressed President George Walker Bush's commission proposal to replace part of Social Security with individuals' private accounts. Other parts of the commission's plan were to increase the retirement age and cut participants' benefits (Report of the President's Commission, 2001). Most literature explored the consequence of replacing the current Social Security system with individual private investment accounts. These studies indicated that workers would support the privatization of Social Security if the system would yield benefits greater than those offered by the current SSA (Barabas, 2006). "Citizens are especially likely to favor Social Security privatization during times of rising stock prices. When domestic equity markets decline, then the support for privatization also declines" (Barabas, 2006, p. 59). Some workers doubt that privatization could be a remedy for the problems of the current Social Security retirement system (Barabas, 2006). Other authors revealed that the privatization of Social Security is too risky because the stock market is unstable (Weller, 2006). In addition, poor people and lower-income workers may have no investment skills to handle the daunting stock market.

There are two schools of thought for the reform of Social Security. Philosophical supporters of personal accounts believe in "ownership" and control of retirement savings, whereas the other school of thought belongs to those who believe in fiscal responsibility. They see personal accounts as an instrument to increase national savings. It is also a way to reduce the burden traditional Social Security will place on future workers and on government finances (Biggs, 2003; Garrett & Rhine, 2005). There are those who argue that workers should be allowed to invest a higher portion of their payroll taxes into personnel savings accounts. One school of thought believes that personal accounts should be used to reduce the growth of Social Security's costs in the short term and over time (Biggs & Springstead, 2008). Fiscal responsibility supporters favor allowing workers to invest a small portion of the total payroll tax. This will enable the government to achieve the goal of keeping "Social Security's finances balanced both over the long term and on a year-to-year basis" (Biggs & Springstead, 2008, p. 2). Biggs (2003) suggested that the plan presented by the President's Commission of 2001 to reform Social Security should be modified to achieve philosophical and fiscal responsibility objectives. The government should increase the personal account size that is available to workers/employees, and greater ownership should be provided along with control and inheritability of payroll taxes. Furthermore, the government should reduce the requirement to transfer unspecified tax revenues over the 75-year period and should also reduce the size of cash shortfalls in any particular year (Biggs, 2003, p. 6).

This modification is necessary to implement a specific policy on individual personal account plans that can be embraced by both philosophical and fiscal responsibility supporters. Changing the current PAYGO to the individual personal accounts plan may be the best solution for Social Security's problems, if other studies support the model.

Several researchers supported the notion that the Social Security program should be restructured to allow private retirement plans (Barabas, 2006; Biggs, 2003; Feldstein, 2007; Ferrara, 1999; Gokhale, 2001, Garrett & Rhine, 2005; Lips, 1998, 1999; Tanner, 2000). Shipman (2003) affirmed that the reform of Social Security would enable workers to contribute to private retirement plans that would be invested in earning assets without using Social Security taxes. Shipman argued that private plans would lead to great rewards if the federal government allowed workers to have the freedom to invest their FICA taxes in financial assets, such as stocks and bonds. History has shown that the investment system would yield higher interest and benefits for workers or investors. For example, if an individual is born in the year 1970 and invests in stocks instead of paying the amount in Social Security taxes, that individual could receive benefits up to six times (as much as $11,729 per month) the benefit received under the Social Security system. Furthermore, even an individual who earns low wages would earn approximately three times the return on Social Security (Shipman, 1995, p. 2). Based on this analysis, individual private accounts, if properly implemented, would enable employers to provide an alternative retirement system to workers that will yield a higher rate of return in investments. The private investment accounts system was not only designed to help rectify Social Security problems; it was also designed to provide long-term sustainable retirement benefits for workers.

PART II

THE DEPTH COMPONENT

Napoleon Imarhiagbe, PhD

Annotated Bibliography

Arnone, W. J. (2006). Are employers prepared for the aging of the U.S. workforce? *Benefit Quarterly, 22*(4), 7–12.

Arnone's (2006) research considered the trend of the aging population in the U.S. workforce. The main purpose of this study was to determine how organizations are responding to the aging workforce. The author used a survey research method to determine how many older workers may be retiring from their organizations over the next 5 to 10 years. The author also examined whether some organizations try retaining older workers after their retirement age. In addition, this study reinforced the notion that life expectancy has increased dramatically in the United States in the past years:

> An American male born in 2000 has an estimated life expectancy of 74 years. For American women, life expectancy is 80 years. Men reaching age 65 have an average life expectancy of an additional 14.8 years; women have an additional 18.6 years. As a result of increase in average life expectancy, the number of Americans aged 65 and over is projected to more than double by the year 2030. (Arnone, 2006, p. 8)

The author revealed that the ages of the baby boomer generation ranged from 42 to 60 in 2006. This represents about one-half of the United States workforce. Within 3 years, "the number of workers ages 45 to 54 will grow by an estimated 21% and the number ages 55 to 64 will grow by over 50%" (Arnone, 2006, p. 8). This trend in the composition of the U.S. older workforce will clearly affect how much benefit individuals will receive from Social Security in the near future.

Barabas, J. (2006). Rational exuberance: The stock market and public support for Social Security privatization. *The Journal of Politics, 68,* 50–61. doi:10.1111/j.1468-2508.2006.00369.x

The author examined individual views pertaining to Social Security privatization. The research revealed that when the stock prices are rising, most people are likely to support Social Security privatization, and people are likely to withdraw their support for privatization when the stock market goes down. The author used different literature reviews to support that position:

> The first empirical analysis shows how an abrupt market decline in 1998 increased opposition to Social Security privatization even after

controlling for individual-level factors. The second study documents a similar relationship over an eight-year period as support for Social Security gradually tracked charge in the stock market. Thus, the public adjusts their preferences for privatization depending upon the direction of the domestic equity markets. (Barabas, 2006, p. 50)

Indeed, people tend to change their attitudes toward the privatization of Social Security based on the conditions of the stock market. The author reinforced the contention that "support for Social Security privatization is conditional on satisfactory signals from the stock markets. If markets drop precipitously, public support for market-based reforms will likely plummet too" (Barabas, 2006, p. 50). The result from this research signifies that the privatization of Social Security may not materialize if the stock market is falling, and the privatization of the Social Security proposal will be implemented if the stock market is booming. Moreover, most people would support the idea if they believe that the program would yield greater benefits than the one provided by the current Social Security system.

Borzutzky, S. (2005). From Chicago to Santiago: Neoliberalism and social security privatization in Chile. *Governance, 18,* 655–674. doi:10.1111/ j.1468-0491.2005.00296.x

The author vigorously explored what led to the idea of the privatization of social security during the dictatorship of Augustine Pinochet in Chile using literature reviews to support what led to the urgent need for reform of Social Security in Chile. The most important reason was that Chile's social security program was in a serious economic crisis. The program discriminated in how benefits were issued to those who were eligible for them. "Pensions for the majority of the blue-collar workers were insufficient because of the combined effect of inflation and the system used to compute the value of pensions" (Borzutzky, 2005, p. 657). Introducing privatization brought equality and fairness to the system and more investment opportunities for workers.

The author also looked at the role of the state and federal governments in the reform of Chile's social security program, demonstrating that social security reform in Chile was used as a political weapon. The program was not only used as a way to strengthen the country's economy, but also as a way to legitimatize the Pinochet regime. "These ideas served to legitimate a political and economic system used in the deprivation of freedom" (Borzutzky, 2005, p. 655).

The late General Pinochet, who took power in a violent coup in Chile, introduced several policies to dismantle his political opponents and those of the former administration who opposed him. One important economic policy he implemented was privatization of the national social security program. The author illustrated that Pinochet's government got the idea of social security privatization from the University of Chicago. The reform of social security was a form of market economy that required regular intervention of the state to guarantee continuous improvement in performance of the market. The success of social security reform in Chile inspired other nations in Latin America to change how their social insurances operated. The author concluded that although Pinochet's regime violated several human and political rights, his government's notion of the privatization of social security should not be undermined.

Burrell, J. (2004). Counterpoint: The case against social security reform. *International Social Science Review, 80*(1&2), 56–59.

The author examined the contention surrounding the Social Security program, arguing that privatization of Social Security is too risky because the market in recent years has been unstable. The author illustrated that

> stock market investment is inherently risky. Stocks go up, and they go down. For every winner there must be a loser. Since Social Security is the only guaranteed income in case of old age or disability, putting Social Security into the stock market would be like betting the rent money. (Burrell, 2004, p. 57)

The author concluded that the privatization of Social Security is a good beginning to reform the system, but the government must be aware of the instability of market investment.

Devroye, D. (2003). Who wants to privatize Social Security? Understanding why the poor are wary of private accounts. *Public Administration Review, 63*, 316–328. doi:10.1111/1540-6210.00292

The author used survey research to demonstrate attitudes toward the privatization of the Social Security program. The author found that the poor are less likely to support the privatization of the Social Security program. Research revealed that poor people trusted the government more to manage the Social Security program than private institutions. Lower income earners and the poor are likely to rely on Social Security as a primary source of income. Poor people prefer to keep their money in the current system rather than invest it. Privatization of the Social Security program may not be able to guarantee or secure taxpayers a minimum level of retirement income. The majority of poor people agreed with the notion that the government should continue to manage the Social Security program because of the risk of privatization.

Estes, C. L. (2004). Social Security privatization and older women: A feminist political economy perspective. *Journal of Aging Studies, 18,* 9–26. doi:10.1016/j.jaging.2003.09.003

The hypothesis of this study was that the Social Security program is unfavorable to "those women who do not conform to the model of family status as married with male breadwinner and those already disadvantaged by race, ethnicity, and class" (Estes, 2004, p. 9). The author found that marital status is one of the factors that increase the poverty rates for older women who were never married, divorced, or separated. The research also revealed that older women who are single have a higher rate of poverty compared to married couples. The author used literature reviews to support this study that Social Security was designed to be more beneficial to the traditional family that has women taking care of the children at home. "In rewarding the increasingly rare 'traditional' nuclear family, state retirement policy may be said to impose a normative and preferential view of family—and one that presently is inherently disadvantageous to the majority of the elderly, older women" (Estes, 2004, p. 12). The author also explicated that there is a great inequality in the Social Security program, based on the way the program was designed to function.

> There is a higher benefit for men than women, for married persons (who are more likely to be male) than unmarried persons (who are more likely to be female), and for dependent spouses than nondependent spouses or single individuals (who are more likely to be women, particularly minority women). (Estes, 2004, pp. 1213)

Korczyk, S. M. (2005). Women's issues in individual social security accounts: Chile, Australia and the United Kingdom. *Benefits Quarterly, 21*(3), 37–47.

The author evaluated President W. Bush's Commission report to strengthen Social Security. The reform's proposed model is based on voluntary individuals' accounts. This research revealed that adding funded individual accounts to the Social Security program will increase retirees' incomes and national saving, and will reduce government budgetary and economic pressures. The author argued that this reform proposal has a potential effect on women. The current population of women receiving Social Security is about 60%, and women are more likely than men to be dependent on Social Security for all or most of their retirement income. The author emphasized that the proposed individuals' voluntary saving accounts should be evaluated carefully because of the impact they will have on women. "Without substantial changes in attitudes and behavior, many women will find it harder to accumulate adequate retirement income through individual accounts than they would in a traditional social insurance program" (Korczyk, 2005, p. 37).

Marmor, T. R. & Mashaw, J. L. (2006). Understanding social insurance: Fairness, affordability, and the 'modernization' of Social Security and Medicare. *Health Affairs, 25,* w114–w134. doi:10.1377/hlthaff.25.w114

The authors analyzed literature reviews on reform of Social Security, arguing that the market system will be adequate for Social Security program reform. "We need to explore the basic structure of social insurance and its capacity to face contemporary challenges, that is, the capacity to modernize while continuing to play its fundamental social role" (Marmor & Mashaw, 2006, p. 115). The authors explicated that privatization will reduce unfairness in the Social Security system, supporting the contention that everyone should be

> putting their Social Security contributions into the stock market then, looking at average returns on common stock over long periods of American history, the analyst demonstrates that the return on these investments would greatly exceed the "return" from social Security contributions." (Marmor & Mashaw, 2006, p. 118)

In contrast, investment in Social Security carries greater risk because of the instability of the stock market. On the other hand, successful investment would enable individuals to generate more funds, which they may not be able to achieve from the current Social Security system. The authors' study supported the contention that most Americans would support privatization of Social Security if it enabled them to raise more funds than the current system would have offered them after their retirement.

Papke, L. E. (2004). Pension plan choice in the public sector: The case of Michigan employees. *National Tax Journal, 57*(2), 329–339. doi:10.17310/ntj.2004.2.10

The author used government records to examine the pension plan of the State of Michigan. The State of Michigan allows public employees with a Defined Benefit (DB) pension plan to transfer vested benefits to an individual account in a portable 401K plan. The author found that new employees are encouraged to enroll in an automatic 401K plan with a mandatory state contribution. Existing employees have the privilege of retaining their current DB. They also have the choice of transferring the present value of their vested pension benefits to a Defined Contribution (DC) plan.

The researcher found that the Michigan State Employee Retirement plan became noncontributory in 1974. In 1997, Michigan stopped offering traditional DB pensions to new state employees. The State now offers only individual DC accounts to newly employed workers.

> The annuity form of DBs is much like Social Security payments. Knowing that part of their retirement incomes from an annuity may incline workers to diversify across types of retirement income and switch to a DC plan where a lump sum payment is an option. On the other hand, the recent discussions of privatizing all or part of Social Security may encourage workers to hang on to a vanishing breed of pension plan. (Papke, 2004, p. 13)

The author compared the DB pension plan in private and public sectors. In the private sector, DB is merely funded by employer contributions (noncontributory plan) whereas in the public sector, the DB plan is mostly founded by employees.

Peters, G. B. (2005). I'm ok, You're (not) ok: The private welfare state in the United States. *Social Policy & Administration, 39,* 166–180. doi:10.1111/j.1467-9515.2005.00432.x

This research revealed that about 200 million Americans have private health insurance. Almost 176 million Americans got their insurance through their employers. The author supported the contention that "private employers provide millions of employee's pension programs either directly or through 401(K) program" (p. 171). Some U.S. employers provide other forms of benefits, such as disability insurance and childcare. The hypothesis is that the "mixture of public and private social provision means that the majority of Americans are members of some public social programs, but for many citizens those public benefits are supplements to their private benefits" (p.167). Private employers provide similar insurance benefits for workers like those of U.S. public employers. Literature reviews supported the position that "although the services provided to American citizens are normally private and corporate, the public sector is really a major player in supporting those services, and in making it possible for businesses to provide services for their employees" (p. 172). Benefit corporations offer employees plans that are deductible from their profits.

Shaw, G., M., & Mysiewicz, S. E. (2006). The polls—Trends: Social Security and Medicare. *Public Opinion Quarterly, 68,* 394–423. doi:10.1093/poq/nfh033

The authors used longitudinal public opinion data on Social Security and Medicare from the mid-1990s to early 2004 to demonstrate why it is necessary to reform the current program. The author found that "Americans continue to be deeply divided on the idea of partial privatization of Social Security, specifically on the idea of individualized investment of a portion of Social Security taxes" (Shaw & Mysiewicz, 2006, p. 394). The majority of the working population opposed the idea of increasing eligibility age or retirement age. The authors used data from Social Security trustees to support the contention that the Social Security program will be in deep trouble within next 2 decades. Most people do not understand the financial problems facing the Social Security program. They do not understand that privatization can help supply solutions to Social Security problems. The reform of Social Security will be very difficult politically, because the majority of the public oppose benefit cuts, eligibility-age increases, or other eligibility limits. However, the majority of the working population will support the privatization of Social Security if it will guarantee more benefits than the ones they would have received from the current system. The authors used data to support the position that 61% of the public would support private investment of Social Security if the plan yielded more benefits (Shaw & Mysiewicz, 2006, p. 394).

Stark, A. Folbre, N., & Shaw, L. B. (Eds.). (2005). Explorations gender and aging: Cross-national contrasts. *Feminist Economics, 11*(2), 163–197. doi:10.1080 /13545700500115985

The article described support systems of the elderly in different countries. The authors found that poverty among elderly women has not been totally eliminated, even in rich industrialized countries. The article revealed that social insurance programs were effective in reducing poverty among elderly women. The authors used comparative analysis to demonstrate that poverty rates among older women were higher than that of men in the United States compared to other industrialized countries. More unmarried older women depend on Social Security benefits to survive in the United States than unmarried older women in other developed countries. Most elderly women depend on family members to support them in the Republic of Korea and the majority of elderly women live with their children. This research pointed out that in most countries, poverty among the elderly (over 75 or older) is far greater when they are living alone. Poverty among the elderly is higher when there is no social security or other governmental programs to support the elderly. The authors concluded that "policy measures are required to relieve the risk of poverty among the elderly, especially women. Strengthening the Old-Age Pension would benefit older women currently" (p.192).

Sutton, T. D. (2005). Economic justice and the future of Social Security. *Human Rights, 32*(2). Retrieved from http://www.americanbar.org/publications/human_rights_magazine_home/human_rights_vol32_2005/summer2005/hr_summer05_socsec.html

The author examined the proposed policy to privatize the Social Security program. Most U.S. workers have social insurance that covers their retirement and disability. Literature reviews led to the position that "30 percent of men and 25 percent of women become disabled before reaching retirement age" (p. 3). Most people are not aware that the public disability insurance program is equal to a private disability policy of $353,000. The argument is that public social insurance is equally as good as private insurance.

Tucker, M. (2002). Partial privatization of Social Security: A simulation of possible outcomes and risks to workers. *Financial Services Review, 11*, 311–326.

This study examined the Bush administration's proposal to privatize Social Security. The author explicated three models for the reform of the Social Security program. The three-model system gives workers the opportunity to invest 4% of their wages in private accounts. Each of the three models includes "a personal savings account that could be invested in a variety of securities, including corporate and treasury bonds as well as equities" (Tucker, 2002, p. 311). The author explained that the three models provide workers with real benefits far greater than those promised under the current system. The author used literature reviews and the President's Commission reports to support the notion that privatization of Social Security would not eliminate the shortfall, but could help reduce the program's deficit.

Whitman, D., & Purcell P. (2006). Income and poverty among older Americans. *Benefits Quarterly, 22*(4), 48–61.

The author examined the current survey on the elderly population receiving retirement benefits. "Retirement benefits from Social Security are the most common source of income among the aged" (Whitman & Purcell, 2006, p. 48). In 2004, 88% of Americans aged 65 and older received Social Security benefits. In the same year, 35% of people aged 65 and older received income from a private or public pension. "Among people aged 65 and older who reported income from a government pension, the median annual amount was $15,600. Among recipients of private pensions, the median amount received in 2004 was just $6,720" (Whitman & Purcell, 2006, p. 48). The authors concluded that although most U.S. senior citizens over 65 receive income from different sources: Social Security benefits, pensions, and income from assets are the most common sources of income.

Introduction

The depth component seeks to explore the economic impact on women, lower income earners, and elders if Social Security is privatized. The main purpose of the Social Security program is to provide a safety net against poverty during old age. The first question to address when evaluating Social Security insurance is whether the program has adequately accomplished its main mission of providing retirement benefits to seniors. What has drawn attention to this issue is that policy makers and social insurance experts continue to speak vigorously about the deficiencies of the current Social Security system. Therefore, it is important that the debate over reform of the Social Security system should consider if privatization of the current system will benefit the majority of American people (Ekaterina & Spiegler, 1998). In addition, will privatization be a good solution for the reform of Social Security and what would be the economic implications for women, lower income earners, and elderly if implemented? In this chapter, a comparative-analysis model is used to analyze different points of view. This discussion will enable policymakers to determine the best solution to reform the Social Security program. This model was also chosen to consider market implications of the Social Security trust fund.

The policy of social insurance was based mainly on poverty alleviation for the elderly. Social Security is a program instituted during the Great Depression to help the weakest and the most vulnerable groups in the United States, especially the poor and elderly. For several years the program has been instrumental in reducing poverty among elderly and poor people. However, recently, Social Security experts, policy analysts, and politicians have questioned whether the program serves its purpose of providing economic support for women, those who are poor, and elders.

Social Security has been criticized by politicians and experts because they believe the program has several major negative impacts on some minority groups, especially the poor, Blacks, women, and the elderly. One reason is that minority groups are compelled to take part in an insurance program that does not suit their interests. Ferrara (1980) demonstrated that "the Social Security program forces everyone in the program to participate in a single insurance program with one set of benefit provisions, provisions that are best suited to circumstance and characteristic of the political powerful majority" (p. 215). As a result, the United States needs social insurance that is diverse and allows each American to choose the program that is best suited to his or her individual circumstances. Based on this notion, it is very important that Social Security be reevaluated to find ways to eliminate the imbalance in the system, which will enable it to meet individual needs, especially those of the elderly, poor, and minorities.

Social Security and Elderly

Social Security has been instrumental in improving the lives of elders over the years. However, the cost of living has also increased dramatically in the past 2 decades. Schulz et al. (1974) demonstrated that "the aged are faced also with rising levels of prices, an economic phenomenon that is almost certain to occur throughout every retirement period" (p. 3). Older people face far greater problems because Social Security benefits may not be enough for them to keep up with the rising cost of living. MaCurdy and Shoven (1999) reinforced the notion that "Social Security benefits are not large enough in and of themselves to support a standard of living in retirement that is equivalent to what beneficiaries achieved during their working lives" (p. 334).

The majority of older citizens are poor and are likely to be in the lower income bracket at the time they retire. Social Security is insufficient for older citizens to support themselves and their families after retirement (MaCurdy & Shoven, 1999). For instance, an elderly individual at the age of 60 who was making $24,000 after taxes and expenses would get about $15,000 annually from Social Security after retirement. By the year 2030, older citizens may need at least $28,000 annually to live comfortably after their retirement, due to inflation (MaCurdy & Shoven, 1999). The number is greater than individuals' original income, if one considers increase in the cost of living. Indeed, reform of Social. Security program is very important to develop an effective system that would generate greater revenues for most elders, enabling the government to improve the lives of most U.S. elderly after their retirement.

Poor and Low-Income Earners

More attention should be paid to the argument made by some experts that Social Security is not meeting its stated goals because the program is unfair to the poor and lower income earners. Social Security taxes hurt the poor more than any other group because individuals with lower incomes pay a greater percentage of their income in taxes. Ferrara's study (1980) found that in 1979, a worker who earned $10,000 paid $1,226 (12.26%) in FICA and a worker who earned $20,000 paid $2,452 (12.26%) in taxes. In contrast, a worker who earned $30,000 paid

$2,807.54 (9.35%), and a worker who earned $40,000 paid $2,809.54 (7.02%) in FICA taxes. Indeed, the percentage of income individuals paid in taxes decreased as wages increased. As a result, poor and low-income earners barely survive on their salaries because of higher taxes. Social Security taxes affect all income levels, but they have a greater impact on the poor:

> It makes little sense to finance the welfare element of Social Security with a regressive payroll. Such a program is plainly counterproductive, with the burden of the tax falling most harshly on the very income groups the program seeks to help. (Ferrara, 1980, p. 220)

Social Security is unfair to lower income earners because of payroll taxes. Indeed, payroll is regressive because it takes a higher percentage of income from those at lower income levels, whereas those at a higher income level pay a lower percentage of taxes. In fact, this tax system hurts those who are already poor and struggling to make a living through their weekly or biweekly paychecks. A vast majority of the poor and lower income earners live from paycheck to paycheck. Researchers (Ferrara, 1980; Tucker, 2002) supported the contention that the tax system does not hurt those who are wealthy and those who have the capacity to pay.

> Income from all other sources, such as capital gains, interest, profits, or other types of investment income are not taxed. Because wages alone constitute a higher proportion of incomes of the poor than those of other income classes, a flat rate tax on wage income will take a higher percentage of income from those with lower incomes than those with higher incomes. (Ferrara, 1980, p. 219)

More importantly, Social Security was designed for the poor to pay more for their benefits and they receive less when eligible for their benefits. One reason is that the working poor tend to start working earlier than those in other income groups in the society. Poor people are likely to start working after graduating from high school. In contrast, middle- and upper-class individuals are likely to attend college after graduating from high school. Most middle- and upper-class people who further their education after high school tend to start full-time work between the ages of 25 and 30. "The poor pay Social Security for several more years than other groups in the society, but paying taxes for these additional years does not earn them any additional benefits" (Ferrara, 1980, p. 216). In addition, most of the time, the money poor people earned before the age of 21 are not included in their benefit calculation. Ferrara also observed that poor people are likely to pay more because there is a higher tax rate for employed workers than those who are self-employed. Without a doubt, people who are self-employed are likely to be wealthier than those who are employed. They are likely to be members of the professional groups who earned higher incomes. More significantly, many low-income workers work 45 years or more, but because Social Security benefits are based on only 35 years of earnings, the extra years are uncompensated (Lips, 1998). Lip (1998) also found that lower income earners and poor people are likely to die earlier. For example, on average, a White man in the highest bracket who reaches the age of 65 will live 3.1 years longer than a White man in the lowest income bracket. Similarly, high-income Black men live 2.5 years longer than do Black men in the lowest income group. Consequently, poor people are likely to receive fewer benefits from Social Security, and they have less time in life to enjoy their benefits (Ferrara, 1980; Lips, 1998).

African Americans and Social Security

As illustrated earlier, the amount of money received from Social Security depends on how long an individual lives (Lips, 1998). As a result, Social Security hurts Blacks more than other racial groups because the life expectancy among them is quite low. The average life expectancy of a Black man born today is just 66.1 years. When a Black man reaches age 65, his payments are less than a White man. A 20-year-old White man can live another 51.6 years, while a Black man is expected to live approximately another 46.8 years. As a result, a Black man is likely to receive approximately 5 years less of benefits than his White counterpart, even though both of them pay the same taxes. In fact, "these benefits represent a much lower return on the taxes paid by blacks than on the taxes paid by white" (Ferrara, 1980, p. 229).

Women and Social Security

Several researchers supported the contention that because Social Security was not well designed, the program is unfavorable to unmarried women (Ekaterina & Spiegler, 1998; Ferrara, 1980; Lips, 1998). A larger population of unmarried people is poor because Social Security is more beneficial to married couples than those who are not married. Ferrara (1980) affirmed that single people are not eligible for additional Social Security benefits like married couples, even though they have paid as much as married people in Social Security taxes.

> Thus, while a single working person will pay the same taxes as a married co-worker with ten children, he will receive nothing from these benefit provisions, while his co-worker can cash in. This single worker must pay for a wife's benefits, although he has no children. He must pay for survivor's benefits that are totally useless to him. The money he pays into the system is used to subsidize his co-worker, who has ten children. (p. 231)

Indeed, Social Security discriminates against women, especially those who work, are childless, and single. The program was designed to favor the traditional family where the husband is the wage earner and the wife is a homemaker or a mother of numerous children. "Those who follow the traditional path receive more in benefits and a greater return on their tax dollar than those who do and those who do not are penalized and forced to subsidize those who do" (Ferrara, 1980, p. 230). Marriage rates have declined and more women are unwilling to get married. More women are choosing to work instead of assuming the traditional homemaking responsibilities. Many married women feel they have to work to support the needs of the family. In addition, divorce rates have increased dramatically. Since the 1930s, women's fertility rates have declined. Women are having smaller families and more are childless. Consequently, unmarried and divorced women are unfairly treated because of the way the current Social Security system was designed.

> Women should be particularly concerned over these inequities because they are part of a system that discriminates against women who work, women who are childless, and women who are single. A single working woman, for example, must pay for all benefit provisions that she does not receive, but a married woman with several children who does not work and pays no taxes may receive benefits on her husband's record for herself and her children when he retires, dies or become disabled. (Ferrara, 1980, p. 232)

Indeed, it is fair to argue that the government uses Social Security taxes for working single women to subsidize married women with children who are not working. Based on the way the Social Security program was designed, a single working woman is discriminated against for choosing to work instead of marry and forced to subsidize those who fit into the traditional mold. Even though a working woman decides to marry, she is still panelized if she has no children.

> If she decides to get married and have children, a penalty may still be exacted if she chooses to work rather than stay home with the children because a wife must forgo the benefit she earns on her own earnings record if she chooses to receive the wife's benefit on her husband's earnings record. (Ferrara, 1980, p. 232)

The SSA encourages women to get married, stay home, and have children. In fact, the program was systemically designed to favor the traditional family. The program discriminates against those women who choose nontraditional lives. Those who do not choose to get married should not be penalized by the system. They should not be compelled to support those who do. People should be responsible for the choices they make in life. "If they wish to get married or have children or forgo working, they should have to pay the costs of doing so, they should not be allowed to impose these costs on others" (Ferrara, 1980, p. 235).

Indeed, Social Security is not well designed because the program systemically discriminates against women by not paying them the same amount of benefit as men, although men and women pay the same taxes (Ferrara, 1980; MaCurdy & Shoven; 1999; Stark et al., 2005). Another problem is that Social Security's provisions are "gender neutral." This is because women's benefits are calculated with the same rules that are used to calculate those for men. The legal equality has led to de facto inequality, due to differences in wages between men and women.

Private Investment and Social Society

One important way to reduce the inequality in the Social Security system is to invest taxes taken from every individual paycheck for Social Security, yielding greater amounts of wealth than would have received from the program. Social Security affects poor people more than other groups because the program induces taxpayers to reduce their savings.

> Without Social Security, taxpayers would be able to save and invest the money they are currently paying into the program, and they would then hold real wealth approximately equal to the present discounted value of future promised Social Security benefits, which can be called Social Security wealth. (Ferrara, 1980, p. 218)

More importantly, the government should put a plan in place that will teach individuals how to manage their money designated for Social Security investment (Ferrara, 1980).

> Social Security will be fair if poor people and other members of society have the opportunity to invest some portion of their income. If each household saved and invested a major portion of its income each year, individual households would begin to accumulate significant amounts of wealth. Each household holds an additional amount of wealth approximately equal to present discounted value of the household's expected future Social Security benefits. (Ferrara, 1980, p. 218)

Individuals' needs would be met if Social Security wealth were equally distributed. In fact, the majority of the working population would be better off if they were allowed to save and invest the amounts they are currently paying in Social Security taxes into private accounts. Ferrara's (1980) study pointed out that by using this plan, the concentration of wealth in the top 1% of the population would be cut in half from 40% to 20% because the majority of the working poor would invest in opportunities like those who are wealthy. Indeed, the 99% of the working poor and low-income earners would be able to accumulate more wealth. The wage gap between the poor and rich is quite high. Indeed, private investment in Social Security would be able to increase income equality in the U.S. (Estes, 2004; Ferrara, 1980; Stark et al., 2005).

Conclusion

The reform of Social Security is necessary now. One can no longer argue that everything is fine with the current Social Security system; the program needs immediate reform for several reasons. The program is unfair to women, lower income workers, Blacks, and elder. In addition, the poor pay more Social Security taxes and receive fewer benefits. Another reason is that by 2030, almost all baby boomers will have retired, and life expectancy at age 65 is projected to be nearly 18 years longer for men and more than 21 years longer for women, indicating more years in retirement and more years receiving Social Security benefits (Social Security Advisory Board, 2001).

The current program provides low-wage employees with a benefit equal to approximately 50% of their preretirement income. Older citizens who rely on Social Security receive just 58% of their income and often fall below the poverty threshold. Social Security's benefits are not enough to rectify the problems of poverty. Most experts believe that to maintain a preretirement standard of living, retirees need between 60 and 85% of their preretirement income (Lips, 1998). Social Security redistributes money from current and future workers to those who are retired, from women to men, from single to married couples, and from two-income families to one-income families. Women and minorities suffer most under the current system, which is not beneficial to them. Women receive lower benefits than men, are punished by divorce, and receive only partial benefits as part of a two-income household. These inequalities in the current system are particularly damaging to women, as they tend to have less independent retirement savings, smaller supplementary pensions, and a longer life span that requires greater savings.

Private investment of Social Security would help eliminate the deficiencies in the present system. With the new development of private savings plans, women can overcome these barriers in the public system and be able to save more for their retirement (Lips, 1998). As low-income individuals rely disproportionately on Social Security, a privatized system offers them more rewarding benefits. In addition, it enables them to accumulate wealth and transfer that wealth between generations, unlike the current system. It is very important to encourage private investments, because privatized Social Security can ease some of the shortcomings of the current distribution of bequeathal wealth. As states by Social Security experts, private investment will reduce income inequality in the current system and will enable lower income workers and minorities to have investment opportunities that are not provided by the current Social Security system.

PART III

APPLICATION COMPONENT

Napoleon Imarhiagbe, PhD

Introduction

As stated in the Breadth and Depth components of this book, Social Security may no longer be meeting the stated goals of providing retirement benefits for workers (Shaw & Mysiewicz, 2006). Therefore, the purpose of the application is to explore deficiencies in Social Security and the impact it will have on workers who retire. The strengths and weaknesses in the privatization of Social Security will also be examined in this chapter. Lessons learned from the Breadth and Depth findings lead to recommendations for policymakers in determining the best way to restructure the system. Furthermore, by using what has been learned from recent research and experiences, recommendations will be made for alternatives to privatization of Social Security.

The comparative-analysis model is essential in this chapter, aiding the ability to decide whether Social Security should be privatized. This model is valuable in considering the Implications of the Market Solution, Advantages in a Market Solution, Disadvantages of the Nonmarket Solution to Social Security Privatization, and Alternatives to Social Security Privatization. Social Security is still at the root of the U.S. social-welfare system. Since the program was enacted in 1935, it continues to be the economic life support for millions of U.S. citizens. However, based on experts' projections, the program may terminate within 20 years. A report made by the Board of Trustees of the Federal Old-Age and Survivor Insurance and Disability Trust Funds also projected that Social Security would be "bankrupt" in the year 2030 if immediate steps are not taken to change the direction of the program. Several researchers (Barrett & Tseng, 2008; Ferrara, 1980; Meyer, 1987) found that the Social Security program is in a deep crisis. In fact, the issue of Social Security reform was one of the important topics debated among the U.S. presidential candidates in 2000, 2004, 2008, and 2012 election campaigns (Barrett & Tseng, 2008). Most policymakers and the news media are paying attention to the issue of Social Security, and most studies have identified the program's problems. However, the plan to reform the Social Security program has not been identified conclusively.

The Breadth and Depth components pointed out various methods to rectify the problems facing the Social Security program. One study demonstrated that the federal government should increase the retirement age to rectify the problems facing Social Security (Ferrara, 1980). Some experts suggested that Social Security benefits should be cut in order to restore the current system to solvency. Gokhale (2001) revealed that "it would take benefit reductions of 26 percent … to keep the program in actuarial balance over the next 75 years" (p. 2). Gokhale argued forcefully that 26% benefit reductions would be too harsh for participants to bear, especially the majority of the poor and elderly who rely more on Social Security benefits. As a result, the benefit-cut plan is unlikely to materialize, due to the impact it would have on the poor and elderly. Some experts suggested that the federal government can sustain the program by reducing military spending and using the savings to fund Social Security. The problem with this idea is that cuts in the military's budget are unforeseeable in the near future because of the ongoing wars in Iraq and Afghanistan including the war on terrorism (Gokhale, 2001).

Another idea to reduce Social Security's budget deficit is that the federal government should increase workers' payroll tax (Gokhale, 2001). According to Tanner (2002), the federal government needs to increase payroll taxes by about $ 103.47 per worker after 2016 at the time the system starts running a deficit. By 2030, the government needs to increase Social Security taxes to $1,543.04 per worker, and it is likely to continue to rise thereafter.

Table 2

Increase Required to Preserve Social Security's Solvency

Year	Taxes per worker ($)	Year	Taxes per worker ($)
2016	103.47	2027	1,312.07
2017	218.12	2028	1,397.35
2018	336.69	2029	1,474.08
2019	457.54	2030	1,543.04
2020	579.91	2031	1,606.49
2021	693.64	2032	1,665.68
2022	806.28	2033	1,715.58
2023	914.51	2034	1,753.08
2024	1,019.93	2035	1,781.23
2025	1,121.66	2036	1,803.52
2026	1,218.52	2037	1,821.61

Note. From *The 2001 Annual Report of the Board of Trustees of the Federal Old-Age and Survivors Insurance and Federal Disability Insurance Trust Funds,* by U.S. Board of Trustees of the Federal Old Age and Survivors Insurance and Disability Insurance Trust funds, 2001, retrieved from https://www.ssa.gov/oact/tr/TR01/

A huge tax increase would have serious consequences for the U.S. economy (Tanner, 2002). In addition, a higher percentage of Social Security payroll taxes is likely to reduce the nation's jobs and economic growth. Tanner's study illustrated the chronology of payroll taxes and consequences. The increase in payroll taxes between 1979 and 1982 led to the loss of 500,000 jobs. Moreover, between 1988 and 1990, payroll-tax hikes resulted in the loss of 510,000 jobs in the United States. This led to a reduction in the U.S. gross domestic product by $39 billion in those years (Tanner, 2002, p. 3). Consequently, the increase in payroll taxes is not healthy for the economy and does not lead to investment opportunities and job growth (Tanner, 2002).

Indeed, any plan to increase Social Security payroll taxes would be controversial because such a plan would be unbearable for poor people. The majority of the public would find it unacceptable to increase Social Security payroll taxes because of the economic conditions in this early 21st century. Gokhale (2001) supported the notion that "the poorest life time earners suffer disproportionately large increases in their lifetime net tax rates under the majority of proposed reforms, for example, a direct tax hike hits the poorest and middle lifetime earners the hardest" (p. 2).

Ferrara (1980) asserted the federal government should seek other avenues to rectify Social Security's problem rather than increasing payroll taxes to generate more funds to finance the program. Tanner (2002) affirmed that it may not be necessary to cut participants' benefits or increase Social Security payroll taxes if workers are given the opportunity to invest a portion of their Social Security taxes in private accounts. An individual investment plan will enable them to save and accommodate wealth. It will also help reduce income equality in the U.S. In addition, it will help to eliminate unfairness in the Social Security system. Privatization of Social Security will enable lower income earners and minorities to save toward their retirements. Some researchers supported the idea that privatization would be the best system to reform the Social Security program because it gives the poor, women, and minorities the opportunity to invest their money—an opportunity not provided by the current system. (Ferrara, 1980; Lips, 1999; Tanner, 2002)

Implications of the Market Solution

Privatization may be an effective way and immediate solution to reforming the Social Security system. As demonstrated earlier, in the near future, a possibility exists that the government will be unable to meet its obligations to retired workers and will have to choose between cutting benefits, raising taxes, and increasing the federal debt. This is not a good idea for the nation's economy and future retirees. This may the reason the government should heed experts' advice to reform the Social Security program as soon as possible.

The proposed reform system would allow workers to redirect their payroll taxes to individually owned, privately invested accounts. The government would give individuals the chance to prefund their future retirement benefits. Through the power of compound interest, all workers would provide benefits significantly greater than those promised by Social Security today. This is very important for low-wage employees who depend heavily "on a stream of income for retirement security" (Lips, 1999, p. 7). Private accounts provide a great reward. The increase in the savings rate would enable the economy to grow, thereby creating more jobs. Indeed, the poor would be self-sufficient, providing themselves a better retirement than the one promised by Social Security. Also, they would not depend on the government for a monthly retirement check. Several researchers reinforced the notion that the poor would benefit most by transforming today's Social Security system into one based on individual saving accounts (Ferrara, 1980; Lips, 1999; Tanner, 2002).

Advantages of a Market Solution

The Social Security system should be privatized for important reasons. The government would give individuals the opportunity to manage their future retirement benefits and accumulate substantial savings by taking advantage of markets. All workers would receive higher retirement benefits under a system that gave them the ability to invest their contributions in productive enterprises (Lips, 1998).

Throughout a worker's lifetime, contributions would accumulate and earn interest in an account. As a result, at retirement, a person's asset would be able to provide a much higher monthly benefit than Social Security.

> Each individual's personal retirement account would be private property, which could be passed onto his heirs at death. [In the present system], a single mother could work and contribute to Social Security for her whole lifetime, and if she died at 64, Social Security would give nothing to pass on to her children. ... With personal retirement accounts, the same woman, born in 1960, making $15,000 a year throughout her lifetime

would, by the time she was 64, accumulate $300,000 in a balance fund that could be left to her descendants. (Lips, 1998, p. 8).

The net gain would be very important to families who are now unable to leave an inheritance to the next generation, and would go a long way toward breaking the cycle of poverty. This system can be fair if it is allowed to be implemented (Lips, 1998).

Disadvantages of the Nonmarket Solution

Any debate of the risk of privatization must also recognize the obvious risks of staying with the present system. As predicted by some experts, the program is underfunded by $9 trillion (Gokhale, 2001). There is a possibility that retired workers' benefits will be cut and workers' taxes will be increased. The SSA reported that by 2032, it would be able to pay only three-quarters of legislated benefits. As a result, future retirees are at great risk (Lips, 1999).

Compare and Contrast

Critics argued that private markets are dangerously risky and that only knowledgeable and experienced investors can successfully handle such risks. According to the Advisory Council on Social Security (1994–1996),

> investors need sophisticated knowledge to invest successfully, sophistication millions of participants in Social Security lack—But many, perhaps, 100 million participants in Social Security, lack requisite knowledge, such as the market served by individual companies, ways of judging the competence of management, relevant changes in technology and whether an individual company is able to keep current, the competitive situation, both local and sometimes international, the company's unfounded promises to pay deferred compensation to highly paid employees, and many other factors. (as cited in Hieger & Shipman, 1997, p. 5)

Turner (2002) disputed the notion that low-income workers are not knowledgeable enough to make investment decisions. For years, workers of all income groups have participated in defined benefit plans, entrusting their pensions to sophisticated investors, who, for the most part, have done very well in fulfilling their obligations. Indeed, in DC plans where individuals have more of the investment responsibility, they have been shown to invest intelligently, when given the opportunity (Turner, 2002).

Alternative Plans to Social Security Privatization

Some states and local governments, such as the San Diego, Galveston County, and the City of New York have their own alternative retirement systems that were substituted for Social Security. Alternative retirement plans introduced by NYC, San Diego, and other local governments give employees the opportunity to save and invest a portion of their incomes. This system allows employees to generate extra income that will be added to their Social Security benefits after their retirements.

In 1981, the City of San Diego made a very important economic decision to opt out of the Social Security program. City administrators believed at that time that the cost of Social Security was going to rise. Administrators contemplated that an independent retirement program could provide a better cost–benefit ratio (Lips, 1999). As a result, the City of San Diego introduced a system called Supplemented Pension Savings Plan (SPSP). This was a mandatory-contributing program that replaced the city employee Social Security program (Lips, 1999).

The SPSP was specifically designed for the City of San Diego's employees, allowing automatic contribution of 3% of their incomes to their SPSP account. Employees hired before July 1986 were allowed to contribute an additional 4.5% of their incomes to their SPSP accounts. Those who were hired after 1986 were given a stipulation that allowed them to contribute an additional 3.05% of their incomes. "The City of San Diego matches 100 percent of the employee's contribution, including the voluntary portion" (Lips, 1999. p. 6).

> As of October 1997, only 161 of the 2 462 participants who were eligible to contribute 4.5 percent of their salaries were not taking full advantage of the opportunity. [Out] of the 5.450 who were eligible to contribute percent, only 893 were not doing so. (Lips, 1999, p. 6)

At the beginning of the program in 1981, all employees' contributions were invested by the City treasurer in low-risk investments such as U.S. government securities and money markets. In October 1996, individuals were able to take over the control of their investment selections. All employees now have the privilege of investing their contributions in a combination of five funds.

> The funds represent various levels of risk. On the low-risk end is the Managed Income Fund, comparable to the Fund Managed by the City treasurer prior to the change in 1996. This fund consists of stable value contracts, primary securities of the United States government. At the high-risk end is the Templeton Foreign fund, which consists primary of non-U.S. stocks. There is also a fund made up primary of stocks from the standard and Poor's (S&P) 500 and a fund that uses a mix of stocks and bonds. (Lips, 1999, p. 6)

The City of San Diego provided every employee with a pamphlet and tapes educating them about how the SPSP program works. It also educates employees about investment strategies and how to avoid riskier stocks and loss of investment. One condition is that workers may not access their accounts until retirement or termination of their employment. Workers may access their retirement funds at the age of 55 if they are eligible. At this age, there is no tax penalty on any amount of loans participants may borrow. Another condition is that workers must have a minimum of 20 years of service. Participants who do not access their accounts at this age can also apply when they reach the age 59.5 (Lips, 1999). According to Lips (1999), participants can also decide not to access their funds and to let the funds continue to grow. When participants die, full payment would be made to their chosen beneficiary (Lips, 1999).

More importantly, San Diego's SPSP market-investment plan provides individuals with a market rate of return on their contributions. A low-risk investment account has a higher rate of return. In fact, it has a record of success, providing an average nominal rate of return of more than 8% over the past 15 years. For example, a worker operating an SPSP account at the of 22 in 1982 contributed a minimum of 6% of a $30,000 salary to a low-risk managed investment fund; at the age of 39 in 1999, the investor would accumulate about $60,000 in a retirement account. Lips (1999) added that in the same year of 1999, the worker would have saved $120,000 for retirement, "if he had taken advantage of a portion of the voluntary option and made a contribution of 12 percent, which is comparable to what he would have paid Social Security" (p. 8). Lips' study (1999) reinforced the position that if a worker has the opportunity to control investment selections, the employee is likely to accumulate wealth far greater than the one Social Security offers. If a worker contributed 12% of salary to an investment account and moved these assets to a fund, the worker would have accumulated up to $150,000 from the investment fund at the time of retirement. Lips (1999) asserted that SPSP offers a greater opportunity for employees to save and accumulate wealth:

> For example, an individual who begins working for the City of San Diego at the 30 and works for 35 years for a salary of $30,000. Assume that he contributes just the minimum to his SPSP account and earns a 7 percent real rate of return (the average real rate for U.S. stocks from 1926 through 1996 was 7.56 percent). At retirement, he would have an account worth more than 266,244 in today's dollars. (Lips, 1999, p. 8)

Based on SPSP estimates, if a male worker retirees at the age of 65 today, he would be receiving a $1,802 monthly payment. With a plan participant, a spouse of the same age with a joint-survivor annuity would be entitled to a $1,565 monthly payment from SPSP.

> If the City employees described above were to take advantage of voluntary contribution and pay closer to what Social Security takes of out of most workers' paychecks, his benefits would be $532,488. According to plan administrator, that could provide a monthly annuity of $3,605 for a single man or a payment of $3,136 that would continue during the lifetime of a spouse of the same age. The more conservative annuity estimate would result in a monthly benefit of approximately $2,052. (Lips, 1999, p. 8)

Based on analysis and comparing SPSP benefits to Social Security, workers who participated in the Social Security program are entitled to $1,077 of monthly benefits after paying 12.4% of their income to the program. Even workers who participate in the SPSP program with a minimum contribution to their accounts would receive more retirement benefits than expected benefits provided by San Diego's SPSP program is a good example of how mandatory systems, based on individuals' investments, can run successfully, and shows how private investment accounts provide rewarding savings to the City's employees and retirees. Indeed, SPSP provides employees the opportunity for employees to have more freedom and control over their own retirements savings, which allows them to be financially secure after their retirements (Lips, 1999).

Napoleon Imarhiagbe, PhD

Galveston County Alternative Plan to Social Security

Galveston County introduced an alternative plan for its employees in 1981 when three counties in Texas decided to withdraw from the Social Security program. In the alternative plan,

> Galveston County employees hired after 1987 contribute 6.13 percent of their earnings to their "retirement annuity accounts," which are administered by a financial services company. The county also contributes 7.785 percent, less the cost of disability and survivor insurance, to participants' accounts. (Lips, 1999, p. 8)

The system was established so that "all mandatory contributions would be invested with a single financial services company in a vehicle with a fixed return" (Lips, 1999, p. 9). This was done to allow investors to avoid financial risks. Lips (1999) stressed that the Galveston Alternative Plan's (GAP) administrator would ensure that the financial company selected would undergo a bidding process. The County's administrators also ensured that contracts were awarded to the company that promised to provide the highest fixed rate of return. There is a condition that allows plan participants to have a lifetime privilege to withdraw the assets in their accounts in case of an emergency beyond their control. Also a condition in the plan requires participants who withdraw their assets before the age of 59.5 to pay a tax penalty (Lips, 1999).

Participants who retire are allowed to use the assets in their accounts for a variety of benefit payments. In addition, it provides payments to a spouse or beneficiary. A retiree can elect to receive a lump-sum payment for the entire amount of assets. GAP also provides rewarding survivor benefits through a life insurance policy to workers. Lips' study (1999) supported the position that the beneficiaries of plan participants, who are under the age of 70, receive 300% of a lump-sum payment of their annual earnings through GAP. They are also entitled to $50,000 of minimum benefit payments and a maximum benefit of $150,000 (p. 9).

Moreover, a plan participant's beneficiary who is 75 or older is entitled to 130% of annual earnings, in addition, to a minimum benefit of $33,330, and a maximum benefit of $100,000 (Lips, 1999). "In addition to this lump-sum payment, the retirement account becomes part of the individual's estate and is transferable to their heirs" (Lips, 1999, p. 9). Workers also have disability-insurance protection. Those who are eligible receive up to 60% of the base payment with the maximum amount the plan offers. The minimum amount of monthly benefit payments is up to $100 (Lips, 1999).

GAP has a substantial number of benefits that far exceed those of Social Security. For example, a plan participant at the age of 65 who has accumulated assets of $320,000 would receive a monthly payment of $2,494 (Lips, 1999). Assuming individuals have a lower benefit plan, they are likely to receive a monthly payment of $2,076 (Lips, 1999, p. 10). By using a conservative annuity estimate, a worker is likely to receive a monthly payment of $1,259. In contrast, a worker who is participating in the Social Security program is only entitled to $1,077 payment from the Social Security Administration (Lips, 1999).

NYC Alternative Plan to Social Security Privatization

Instead of privatization, workers can also save money toward their retirements by using a plan similar to the New York City Deferred Compensation Plan or the 401K system. The City of New York's Deferred Compensation Board was founded on April 16, 1985 by Executive Order No. 81 of the Office of the Mayor. Board members include the mayor of the City of New York, Comptroller of the City of New York, Director of the Office Management & Budget, Commissioner of Finance, Commissioner of the Office of Labor Relations, Commissioner of Citywide Administration Services, and corporate counsel. The board enacted the Deferred Compensation Plan (457) in 1986, governed by S457 of the Internal Revenue Code of 1986 for the City's employees. (City of New York Comptroller, 2007). The Deferred Compensation Plan (457) Board indicated in the policy that

> the Participation Agreement must specify a) the percentage of the participant's compensation to be deferred in multiples of 0.5%, not less than 1% nor greater than 50% and b) the investment option(s) selected by the participant, including the percentages to be allocated to the selected option(s), in investments of 1%. (The New York City Deferred Compensation Plan/New York City Employee IRA Comprehensive Annual Financial Report, 2006, p. 8)

In this plan, employees are allowed to deduct some percentages of their biweekly income from payroll. "[They] do not pay income taxes on their contributions or investment returns while these funds remain in the plans" (The New York City Deferred Compensation Plan/New York City Employee IRA Comprehensive Annual Financial Report, 2006, p. 8). The 457 plans give workers the opportunity to borrow money from their contributions or accounts for emergency use or any other reasons. This plan is a voluntary retirement program that was developed by the City to generate extra revenues for workers after or before their retirements.

The federal government can introduce a system called a federally Deferred 402k system. This is not a voluntary deduction program unlike the 401k. In this plan, 5% of the biweekly payroll is automatically deducted from employees making less than $60,000 annually. For example, a worker with annual salary of $20,000 can save up to $50,000 when retiring at the age of 65 (New York City Deferred Compensation Plan, 2006).

Recommendations

About 22 years ago, the federal government took one important step in reforming the Social Security program. In May 2001, President Bush established a commission to strengthen Social Security. A report released by the commission warned that the current Social Security system may not be able to meet the needs of future retired workers. The commission pointed out that the current Social Security system needs overhaul because it is unsustainable, based on its current structure. As a result, the commission introduced three types of Social Security reform (Report of the President's Commission, 2001).

All three models allow one to establish a voluntary investment account. Model I offered a personal private account, but included no other changes to Social Security benefits to obtain long-term maintenance of the program. Model II offers solvency without increasing taxes. This model does not require workers to make additional contributions toward their benefits. The most important part of this model is that it achieves solvency. It will also enable the federal government to balance Social Security revenues and costs. Under Model II, workers would be allowed to invest about 4% of their payroll in a private account up to $1000 per year, and 2% thereafter (Weller, 2006). Model III offers room for one to exceed current benefits and wage-replacement ratios (Report of the President's Commission, 2001).

Many Social Security experts asserted that Model II is a reasonable plan because it offers workers an investment opportunity to generate more income for their retirement. Nearly all workers would invest in the program, because the contribution is voluntary and is subsidized. One major change in Model II is that new retirees' benefits would no longer increase at the rate of employees' wages, but would grow only at the rate of inflation (Weller, 2006). Moreover, workers would have the advantage of borrowing from their private accounts and the choice of paying for the loan after their retirement. Another advantage is that a personal account would enable the federal government to generate more revenue, which would lead to an increase in national savings. Indeed, the implementation of a personal account is essential, because it would enhance retirement security (Report of the President's Commission, 2001).

U.S. policymakers should consider implementation of a personal-investment account. As noticed by the Social Security's commission, many countries have changed their retirement plans to a personal account, including Chile, Australia, Mexico, Poland, Switzerland, and the United Kingdom. China and Russia are in the process of implementing a personal account. Even Sweden, a country that offers generous public retirement benefits to employees, is contemplating changing to a private personal retirement plan (Report of the President's Commission, 2001). Chile particularly faced retirement crises, similar to the United States, until the government introduced private investment accounts. In the late 1970s, Chile's retirement system was facing bankruptcy and lacked savings. The pay-as-you-go format was inadequate and flawed. The reform of Chile's traditional social security to a private investment-account system turned the program into a productive enterprise. Indeed, the new private investment account plan has been remarkably successful. The success of Chile's private account system has been credited with giving workers the privilege of contributing 10% of their salaries to their own accounts at a Pension Fund Company known as Administadoras de Fondos de Pensiones (AFP). AFP assists workers by investing their contributions in securities such as stocks and bonds. Workers' contributions and investment returns are not taxed. However, any withdrawal made by workers is taxed (Shipman, 1995).

Since the system became fully operational in May 1981, workers' retirement benefits have doubled.

> Worker's average rate of return on investment has been 14 percent per year. As a result, the typical retiree is receiving a benefit equal to nearly 80 percent of his average annual income over the last 10 years of his working life, almost double the U.S. replacement value. (Shipman, 1995, p. 12)

As of 1995, workers' investment accounts managed by AFP accumulated about $23 billion, which is about 41% of the country's gross domestic product (Shipman,

1995). Chile's real gross domestic product has achieved tremendous growth for the past 2 decades. It has an average growth of over 6%, which is far greater than that of the United States. Shipman (1995) demonstrated that between 1989 and 1994, the annualized total return of the Chilean stock market was 48.6% versus 8.7% for the United States. This is remarkable success for any country's private retirement investments and growth.

The Social Security's commission also observed that the U.S. government would be lagging behind if it does not follow the footsteps of other countries in modernizing its Social Security retirement system. Copying from the international experience and the Social Security commission's report, a private personal account plan could be a cost-effective way of administering Social Security and could also be a way of increasing workers' retirement benefits (Report of the President's Commission, 2001).

If this is the case, policymakers should revisit the notion of personal private-investment accounts. Although there are some bona fide ideas in the commission's report to fix the problems facing the Social Security program, the commission's recommendations were never reviewed by the House committee or debated by congressional members, nor were they enacted into law. What made the commission's report important is that it included several outside experts' views and research supporting personal-investment accounts. Therefore, the report should not continue to be ignored by lawmakers, and should be reevaluated to see if there are any adjustments that need to be made to the recommendation. In fact, there should be public debate regarding these recommendations and other experts' solutions to rectify the program's problems (Report of the President's Commission, 2001).

The public must be educated on why Social Security program reform is necessary. They must understand possible reforms, including how they may be implemented and administered and how the new changes would affect their retirement benefits. (Robertson 1985). The public must remain informed about how they can manage their money in the future. "It is important that all reform proposals require some additional outreach to the public so that future beneficiaries can adjust their retirements planning accordingly" (Walker, 2003, p. 17).

Conclusion

The researchers and policymakers cannot overlook reform of the Social Security program. Breadth and Depth research components demonstrated that in the near future, the government may be unable to meet its obligations to retired workers and will have to choose between cutting benefits, raising taxes, and increasing the federal debt. Based on the Depth study, putting off the decision is not a good idea for the nation's economy and the future retirees, especially for low-income workers and minorities (Lips, 1998). In fact, tax increases and benefit cuts may not be able to rectify the problems facing the Social Security program, and may not lift the poor out of poverty. A private system provides them with greater opportunities to ensure a stable and self-generated retirement.

Breadth and Depth research findings also revealed that low-income workers have shorter life expectancies than wealthier Americans, and thus receive a smaller share of their current benefits packages. Indeed, with private accounts, unspent savings can be accumulated by younger generations, thereby helping to create a foundation for future fiscal stability. Privatizing the Social Security program offers a new way to provide a better retirement for all Americans through a supportable long-term program. Undoubtedly, moving away from the publicly funded system will enable the federal government to avoid the impending failure of the trust fund. At the same time, it evades the unpleasant options of raising taxes and cutting benefits.

Alternatives to Social Security privatization are important options policymakers should consider to reform the system because they have a greater chance of benefiting the poor, women, minorities, and other citizens. Providing alternative plans to workers would enable the federal government to put the inefficient system in order and diminish the controversy surrounding the proposed Social Security privatization. More importantly, it would enable the government to reduce the income inequality in the Social Security system. Poor households and lower income workers barely save toward their retirements and may not be able to survive on Social Security checks after their retirement. Gokhale (2001) reinforced this position that alternatives to privatization of the Social Security program "may provide an opportunity to address some of the other problems with the current Social Security system, in particular its impact on wealth accumulation, the intergenerational transfer of wealth in America (p. 1).

The federal government should support alternative plans to Social Security privatization for good reasons. For examples, the SPSP, GAP, and the New

York City Deferred Compensation Plan give workers investment opportunities that enable them to generate additional income after their retirements. Workers would receive a return from their investments that is far greater than what they could have received from the SSA. Workers would no longer worry about experts' projections that the Social Security program would be bankrupt within 20 years if there were an alternative plan to save and invest their money.

PART IV

EMPIRICAL RESEARCH

Napoleon Imarhiagbe, PhD

Empirical Research Related to This Study

This section presents the empirical study related to the reformation of the Social Security system of the United States. In response to the Social Security financing crisis that occurred 2 decades ago, the government increased the normal retirement age for people born since 1938. The retirement age for those people began in the year 2000. Mastrobuoni (2006) conducted a study to examine the effect of the recent cuts to benefits. The study found that if the number of older workers continues to increase, significant implications ensue on the sustainability of the Social Security trust fund. The fund will head toward exhaustion and will require the Social Security system to be reformed. Another study by Altig and Gokhale (1997) found that, as the problems and challenges of the Social Security program increase and become more apparent, they will generate a need to privatize the Social Security program. The researchers propose a privatized system and its adoption and implementation process. However, to benefit from it, the proposed plan is valid for workers who are under the age of 32. If these workers shifted to a private social security system, it would divert 40 % of their income taxes to their accounts. Moreover, if the privatization plan was delayed and did not start working before 2011, then workers would only get 22.1% of their income taxes in benefits. Therefore, Altig and Gokhale (1997) suggested that the system be adopted urgently to gain maximum benefit from it.

According to Maroney, Jackson, Rupert, and Zhang (2011), the United States faces exceptionally large budget deficits over the foreseeable future that threatens the nation's financial stability. A large portion of these deficits is due to the Social Security and Medicare programs. Thus, given the likely need to reform these programs, the study used a model of rational choice proposed by Margolis (1981, 1984) and conducted an experiment to determine if the accounting information provided about the Social Security system affects taxpayers' acceptance of reform. The study found that participants who receive accrual-basis financial information are more concerned about the sustainability of the system and, most important, are willing to accept a greater share of the burden of reforming the Social Security system than participants receiving cash-basis financial information and participants in the control condition. However, through supplemental analyses, the researchers found that if the survival of the Social Security system is placed into question, the willingness to sacrifice begins to decline.

Another research study conducted by Kitao (2011) suggested four policy options to reform the Social Security system and make it sustainable in the future. These four options were based on the demographic shift affecting the Social

Security system and included (a) a one-third reduction in replacement rates of the benefit formula, (b) a 6% increase in payroll taxes, (c) taking a means-test of Social Security benefits and reducing them one-to-one with income, and (d) raising the retirement age from 66 to 73. Although these policies had the same objective, their economic benefits differed. Options a and b encourage savings. The increase in payroll taxes in Option b would discourage work effort, and Option c yields the most marked labor disincentives, in particular for the elderly. However, Options a and d were considered the best options (Kitao, 2011). A study conducted by Leidy for the International Monetary Fund in 1997 examined the distributional and macroeconomic consequences of a policy change, while keeping all other things equal, which could lead to U.S. Social Security trust fund assets being invested in private securities. The study found that improving the expected annual return to Social Security trust fund assets through a shift from government bonds to private securities would yield an increase in the future claims available to the working population. The effect on saving and future economic output depends on how current workers interpret the effect of policy change on their future Social Security benefits (Leidy, 1997).

BIBLIOGRAPHY

AARP. (2001). *Keeping Social Security solvent*. Retrieved from http://www.aarp.org/social security/issues/solvent.html

Abdnor, L. (2004). *Social Security choices for the 21st century woman* (SSP No. 33). Retrieved from http://object.cato.org/sites/cato.org/files/pubs/pdf/ssp33.pdf

AC Nielsen Economic. (2005). *More Americans living paycheck to paycheck*. New York, NY: Author.

Acomb, D. L. (2005). Social Security. *National Journal, 26*(37), 2084.

Altig, D., & Gokhale, J. (1997). *Social Security privatization: One proposal* (SSP No. 9). Retrieved from http://www.cato.org/publications/social-security-choice-paper/social-security-privatization-one-proposal

Amable, B. (2003). *The diversity of modern capitalism*. Oxford, England: Oxford University Press.

Amable, B., & Palombarini, S. (2005). *L'économie politique n'est pas une science morale* [Political economy is not a science of morality]. Paris, France: Raisons d'Agir.

Amable, B., & Palombarini, S. (2009). A neorealist approach to institutional change and the diversity of capitalism. *Socio-Economic Review, 7,* 123–143. doi:10.1093/ser/mwn018

American Academy of Actuaries. (2002). *Raising the retirement age for Social Security*. Washington, DC: Author.

Andrews, E. L. (2004, December 16). Bush puts Social Security at top of economic conference. *The New York Times*. Retrieved from http://www.nytimes.com/2004/12/16/politics/bush-puts-social-security-at-top-of-economic-conference.html?_r=0

Anrig, G., & Wasow, B. (2005). *Twelve reasons why privatizing Social Security is a bad idea* (Report No. 18). Retrieved from http://www.tcf.org/work/social_insurance/detail/twelve-reasons-why-privatizing-social-security-is-a-bad-idea

Apfel, K. S. (2000). *Fast facts & figures about Social Security*. Washington, DC: Social Security Administration Office of Policy, Office of Research, Evaluation, and Statistics.

Apgar, W., & Di, Z. X. (2005). *Housing wealth and retirement savings: Enhancing financial security for older Americans* (Working paper W05-8). Cambridge, MA: Harvard University Joint Center for Housing Studies.

Arnone, W. J. (2006). Are employers prepared for the aging of the U.S. workforce? *Benefit Quarterly, 22*(4), 7–12.

Babbie, E. (2007). *The practice of social research* (7th ed.). Sidney, Australia: Thomson & Wadsworth.

Baker, D., & Weisbrot, M. (1999). *Social Security: The phony crisis*. Chicago, IL: The University of Chicago Press.

Ball, C. A. (2005). Chile: Reform success south of the border. *Human Events, 1*, 2–74.

Barabas J. (2006). Rational exuberance: The stock market and public support for Social Security privatization. *The Journal of Politics, 68*(1), 50–61.

Barabas, J. (2006). Rational exuberance: The stock market and public support for Social Security privatization. *The Journal of Politics, 68*, 50–61. doi:10.1111/j.1468-2508.2006.00369.x

Barrett, G. F., & Tseng, Y. (2008). Retirement saving in Australia. *Canadian Public Policy Journal, 34*, S177–193. doi:10.3138/cpp.34.Supplement.S177

Bartels, L. M. (2002). Beyond the running tally: Partisan bias in political perceptions. *Political Behavior, 24*, 117–150. doi:10.1023/A:1021226224601

Baumgartner, F., & Bryan, J. (2002). *Policy dynamics*. Chicago IL: University of Chicago Press.

Becker, F. W. (2007). Reactions to Social Security retirement reform proposals in the United States. *International Social Security Review, 60,* 101–114. doi:10.1111/j.1468-246X.2007.00262.x

Becker, G. S. (1983). A theory of competition among pressure groups for political influence. *Quarterly Journal of Economics, 98,* 371–400. doi:10.2307/1886017

Becker, G. S., & Mulligan, C. (1998). *Deadweight costs and the size of government* (NBER Working Paper No. 6789). Cambridge, MA: The National Bureau of Economic Research.

Berger, J. (1982). *Saving Social Security*. New York, NY: H. W. Wilson.

Biggs, G. A. (2003). *Large accounts and small cash deficits: Increasing personal account size within a fiscally responsible Social Security reform framework* (Social Security Choice Paper No. 30). Retrieved from http://www.cato.org/publications/social-security-choice-paper/large-accounts-small-cash-deficits-increasing-personal-account-size-within-fiscally-responsible-social-security-reform-framework

Biggs, G. A. (2009). Retirement math. *Forbes, 183*(7), 1–2.

Biggs, G. A., & Springstead, G. R. (2008). Alternate measures of replacement rates for social security benefits and retirement income. *Social Security Bulletin, 68*(2), 1–19. Retrieved from https://www.ssa.gov/policy/docs/ssb/v68n2/v68n2p1.html

Blake, D., & Turner, J. (2007). Individual accounts for Social Security reform: Lessons from the United Kingdom. *Benefits Quarterly, 3*(2), 55–60. Retrieved from http://www.pensions-institute.org/workingpapers/wp0707.pdf

Boadway, R. W., & Wildasin, D. E. (1989). A median voter model of Social Security. *International Economic Review, 30,* 307–328. doi:10.2307/2526649

Bolderson, H., & Mabett, D. (1991). *Social policy and social security in Australia, Britain and the USA*. Aldershot, England: Avebury Academic.

Books LLC. (2010). *Quantitative research: Statistical survey, quantitative marketing research, Amba Research, quantitative history, labour force survey.* Memphis, TN: General Books.

Borzutzky, S. (2005). From Chicago to Santiago: Neoliberalism and social security privatization in Chile. *Governance, 18,* 655–674. doi:10.1111/j.1468-0491.2005.00296.x

Bosworth, B. P., Bryant, R. C., & Burtless, G. (2004). *The impact of aging on financial markets and the economy: A survey* (Report No. 58). Washington, DC: Brookings Institution.

Boswoth, B., & Burtless, G. (2000). *The effects of Social Security reform on saving, investment, and the level and distribution of worker well-being* (Report No. 200-02). Chestnut Hill, MA: Center for Retirement Research—Boston College.

Bovbjerg, B. (1998). *Social Security reform: Raising retirement ages improves program solvency but may cause hardship for some.* Washington, DC: Government Printing Office.

Bowerman, B. L., & O'Connell, R. T. (1987). *Time series forecasting: United concepts and computer implementation* (2nd ed.). Boston, MA: Duxbury Press.

Breyer, F., & Craig, B. (1997). Voting on social security: Evidence from OECD countries. *European Journal of Political Economy, 13,* 705–724. doi:10.1016/S0176-2680(97)00031-1

Brown, J. R. (2005). The case for pre-funding Social Security. *Generations, 29*(1), 53–58.

Browning, E. (1975). Why the social insurance budget is too large in a democracy. *Economic Inquiry, 13,* 373–388. doi:10.1111/j.1465-7295.1975.tb00255.x

Browning, E. S. (2005, May 5). As boomers retire, a debate: Will stock prices get crushed? *The Wall Street Journal.* Retrieved from https://www.google.com/url?sa=t&rct=j&q=&esrc=s&-source=web&cd=2&ved=0ahUKEwjZmuCHlc3KAhXHVz-4KHYXmB_cQFgghMAE&url=http%3A%2F%2Fwww.jeremysiegel.com%2Findex.cfm%3Ffuseaction%3DResources.Download%26resourceID%3D6415&usg=AFQjCNFrVN8wjGh5kq86SSg4jk12bqFoNQ

Bryant, C. (2005). Policy point-counterpoint: Social Security reform. *International Social Science Review, 80*(1&2), 51–59.

Burdick, C., & Manchester, J. (2003). Stochastic models of the Social Security trust funds. *Social Security Bulletin, 65*(1), Art. 3. Retrieved from https://www.ssa.gov/policy/docs/ssb/v65n1/v65n1p26.html

Burgoon, B., Demetriades, P., & Underhill, G. (2008). *Financial liberalisation and political variables: A response to Abiad and Mody* (Working Paper 08/30). Leicester, England: University of Leicester Discussion Paper in Economics.

Burrell, J. (2004). Counterpoint: The case against social security reform. *International Social Science Review, 80*(1&2), 56–59.

Burtless, G. (2004). Social norms, rules of thumb, and retirement: Evidence for rationality in retirement planning. In K. W. Schaie, L. L. Cartensen (Eds.), *Social structures, aging, and self-regulation in the elderly* (pp. 123–160). New York, NY: Springer.

Butrica, B. A., Iams, H. M., & Smith, K. E. (2004). The changing impact of social security on retirement income in the United States. *Social Security Bulletin, 65*(3). Retrieved from https://www.ssa.gov/policy/docs/ssb/v65n3/v65n3p1.html

Caffrey, A. (2005, April 3). Can you manage your own money? Amid push to privatize Social Security, many in US admit they're daunted or don't know investment basics. *Boston Globe*, p. K1.

Campbell, D., & Mungan, K. (2007). The security of a guarantee. *Benefits Quarterly, 23*(2), 37–41.

Caputo, R. K. (2008). Personal retirement accounts & the American welfare state: A study of income volatility and social economic status as correlates of PRA support. *Journal of Poverty, 12,* 229–250. doi:10.1080/10875540801973625

Carlos, B. A. (2005). Chile: Reform success south of the border. *Human Events, 1,* 2–74.

Cerda, R. A. (2005). On social security financial crisis. *Journal of Population Economics, 18,* 509–517. doi:10.1007/s00148-005-0233-6

Chen, Y. P. (1980). *Social Security in a changing society. An introduction to programs, concepts, and issues.* Bryn Mawr, PA: McCahan Foundation.

City of New York Comptroller. (2007). *The City of New York Deferred Compensation Plan/New York City Employee IRA Comprehensive Annual Financial Report.* Retrieved from http://comptroller.nyc.gov/reports/nyc-fiduciary-funds-financial-statement

Clark, G. L., & Knox-Hayes, J. (2007). Mapping UK pension benefits and the intended purchase of annuities in the aftermath of the 1990s stock market bubble. *Transactions of the Institute of British Geographers, 32,* 539–555. doi:10.1111/j.1475-5661.2007.00277.x

Clark, G. L., & Monk, A. H. B. (2008). Conceptualizing the defined benefit pension promise: Implication from a survey of expert opinion. *Benefits Quarterly, 1,* 7–20. Retrieved from http://papers.ssrn.com/sol3/papers.cfm?abstract_id=1004743

Claude, J. (2005). Bush's social security plan: Gambling away the nest-egg. *The Black Scholar Journal, 35*(1), 21–25.

Clive, C. (2004). Privatizing social security: An idea whose time has passed. *National Journal, 36*(40), 53–197.

Cohen, J., Cohen, P., West, S. G., & Aiken, L. S. (2003). *Applied multiple regression/correlation analysis for the behavioral sciences.* Mahwah, NJ: Erlbaum.

Congleton, R. D., & Shughart, W., II. (1990). The growth of Social Security: Electoral push or political pull? *Economic Inquiry, 28,* 109–132. doi:10.1111/j.1465-7295.1990.tb00806.x

Congressional Budget Office. (2001). *Social Security: A primer.* Retrieved from http://www.cbo.gov/ftpdocs/32xx/doc3213/EntireReportpdf

Congressional Budget Office. (2009, August). *CBO's long term projections for Social Security: 2009 update.* Retrieved May, 2011, from https://www.cbo.gov/sites/default/files/111th-congress-2009-2010/reports/08-07-socialsecurity_update.pdf

Congressional Budget Office. (2010, August). *CBO's 2010 long term projections for Social Security*. Retrieved from https://www.cbo.gov/sites/default/files/111th-congress-2009-2010/reports/10-22-socialsecurity_chartbook.pdf

Constantinides, G. M., Donaldson, J. B., & Rajnish, M. (2004). Junior must pay: Pricing the implicit put in privatizing Social Security. *Annals of Finance, 1*, 1–34. doi:10.1007/s10436-004-0002-7

Cooper, D. R., & Schindler, P. S. (2003). *Business research methods* (8th ed.). New Delhi, India: Tata McGraw Hill.

Cooper, D., & Schindler, P. (2006). *Business research methods* (9th ed.). New York, NY: McGraw-Hill Higher Education.

Copeland, C. (2006). Individual account retirement plans: An analysis of the 2004 survey of consumer finances. *Employee Benefit Research Institute Notes, 293*, 1–29.

Creswell, J. (2002). *Educational research: Planning, conducting, and evaluating quantitative and qualitative research*. Saddle Upper River, NJ: Pearson Education.

Creswell, J. (2005). *Educational research* (2nd ed.). Upper Saddle River, NJ: Pearson Education.

Creswell, J. (2007). *Qualitative inquiry & research design: Choosing among five approaches* (2nd ed.). Thousand Oaks, CA: Sage.

Daniels, B. (2004). Helping tomorrow's retirees manage: Distribution phase risks. *Benefits Quarterly, 20*(4), 57–60.

Dattalo, P. (2007). Borrowing to save: A critique of recent proposals to partially privatize social security. *Social Work, 52*, 233–242. doi:10.1093/sw/52.3.233

David, J. C. (2005). What do almost 40 countries know that we don't? *Human Events, 2*, 22.

Davidson, A. B., & Ekelund, R. B., Jr. (1997). The medieval church and rents from marriage market regulations. *Journal of Economic Behavior & Organization, 32*, 215–245. doi:10.1016/S0167-2681(96)00903-1

Davies, M. (2007). *Doing a successful research project: Using qualitative or quantitative methods.* New York, NY: Palgrave Macmillan.

Devroye, D. (2003). Who wants to privatize Social Security? Understanding why the poor are wary of private accounts. *Public Administration Review, 63,* 316–328. doi:10.1111/1540-6210.00292

Diamond, P. (2000a). *Towards an optimal Social Security design* (Working Paper 4/2000). Turin, Italy: Center for Research on Pensions and Welfare Policies.

Diamond, P. (2000b). What stock market returns to expect for future? *Social Security Bulletin, 63*(2), 7–11. Retrieved from http://economics.mit.edu/files/637

Diamond, P., & Geanakoplos, J. (2003). Social Security investment in equities. *The American Economic Review, 93,* 1047–1074. doi:10.1257/000282803769206197

Diamond, P., Lindeman, D. C., & Young, H. (Eds.). (1996). Social Security: What role for the future? *proceedings of the Seventh Conference of the National Academy of Social Insurance.* Washington, DC: Brookings Institution Press.

Diamond, P. A., & Orszag, P. R. (2003). *Reforming Social Security: A balanced plan* (Policy Brief 8). Washington, DC: Brookings Institute.

Disney, R., Emmerson, C., & Wakefield, M. (2008). Pension provision and retirement savings: Lessons from the United Kingdom. *Canadian Public Policy, 34,* 155–176. doi:10.3138/cpp.34.4.S155

Dotsey, M. (1997). Investing in equities can it help social security? *Economic Quarterly, 83*(4), 49–69. Retrieved from https://www.richmondfed.org/-/media/richmondfedorg/publications/research/economic_quarterly/1997/fall/pdf/dotsey.pdf

Dreher, W. A. (2005). Society's insurance: One actuary's perspective on strengthening our national retirement system. *Benefits Quarterly, 4*(3), 48–53.

Drutman, L. (2004). A 2005 item: Social Security privatization. *Multinational Monitor, 25*(5/6), 33–35.

Dwyer, G. P., Jr. (2005). Social security private accounts: A risky proposition? *Economic Review, 90*(3), 1–13. Retrieved from https://www.frbatlanta.org/-/media/Documents/research/publications/economic-review/2005/vol90no3_dwyer.pdf?la=en

Ekaterina S., & Spiegler, P. (1998). The benefits of Social Security privatization for women (SSP No. 12). Retrieved from http://www.cato.org/pubs/ssps/ssp12.html

Ekelund, R. B., Jr., & Tollison, R. D. (2001). The interest theory of government. In W. F. Shughart & L. Razzolini (Eds.), *The Elgar Companion to public choice* (pp. 357–378). Northampton, MA: Edward Elgar.

Elmendorf, D. W., Liebman, J. B., Shapiro, M. D., & Zeldes, S. P. (2000). *Social Security reform and national savings in an era of budget surpluses.* Washington, DC: Brookings Institution Press.

Estes, C. L. (2004). Social Security privatization and older women: A feminist political economy perspective. *Journal of Aging Studies, 18,* 9–26. doi:10.1016/j.jaging.2003.09.003

Ezra, D. (2005). Retirement income guarantees are expensive. *Financial Analysts Journal, 61*(6), 74–77. doi:10.2469/faj.v61.n6.2773

Feldstein, M. (2007). *Privatizing Social Security: The $10 trillion opportunity.* Retrieved from http://www.cato.org/publications/social-security-choice-paper/privatizing-social-security-$10-trillion-opportunity

Feldstein, M., & Liebman, J. (2000). *The distributional effects of an investment-based social security system* (NBER Working Paper No. 7492). Cambridge, MA. National Bureau of Economic Research.

Feldstein, M., Ranguelova, E., & Samwick, A. (1999). *The transition to investment-based social security when portfolio returns and capital profitability are uncertain* (NBER Working Paper No. 7016). Cambridge, MA. National Bureau of Economic Research.

Feldstein, M., & Samwick, A. (2000). *Allocating tax revenue to personal retirement accounts to maintain social security benefits and the payroll tax rate* (NBER Work Paper No. 7767). Cambridge, MA: National Bureau of Economic Research.

Ferrara, P. (1980). *Social security: The inherent contradiction*. San Francisco, CA: Cato Institute.

Ferrara, P. (1997, April 30). *A plan for privatizing Social Security*. Retrieved from http://www.cato.org/pubs/ssps/ssp8.html

Ferrara, P. (1999, November 29). *Social Security is still a hopelessly bad deal for today's workers*. Retrieved from http://www.socialsecurity.org/pubs/ssps/ssp-26es.html

Fisher, T. L. (2007). Measuring the relative importance of social security benefits to elderly. *Social Security Bulletin, 67*(2), 65–75. Retrieved from https://www.ssa.gov/policy/docs/ssb/v67n2/v67n2p65.html

Forman, E., & Selly, M. A. (2001). *Decision by objectives (How to convince others that you are right)*. Washington DC: The George Washington University.

Foster, A. C. (1997). Public and private sector defined benefit pension: A comparison. *Compensation and Working Conditions, 1*, 37–42. Retrieved from http://www.bls.gov/mlr/cwc/public-and-private-sector-defined-benefit-pensions-a-comparison.pdf

Friedman, M. (1999). *Speaking the truth about Social Security reform*. Retrieved from http://www.cato.org/publications/briefing-paper/speaking-truth-about-social-security-reform

Galasso, V. (2006). The U.S. Social Security System: What does political sustainability imply? *Review of Economic Dynamics, 2*, 698–730. doi:10.1006/redy.1998.0049

Garrett, T. A., & Rhine, R. M. (2005). Social Security versus private retirement accounts: A historical analysis. *Federal Reserve Bank of St. Louis Review, March/April*, 103–121.

Gatti, D. (2009). Ownership concentration, employment protection and growth. A case for interdependent time-evolving institutions. In J. P. Touffut (Ed.). *Does company ownership matter?* (pp. 49–76). Northampton, MA: Edward Elgar.

Gatti, D., Rault, C., & Vaubourg, A. (200911). Unemployment and finance: How do financial and labour market factors interact? *Oxford Economic Papers, 64,* 464–489. doi:10.1093/oep/gpr046

Gokhale, J. (2001). *The impact of social security reform on low-income workers.* Retrieved from http://www.cato.org/publications/social-security-choice-paper/impact-social-security-reform-lowincome-workers

Gokhale, J. (2010). *Social Security: A fresh look at policy alternatives.* Chicago IL: University of Chicago Press.

Gold, A., & Vorchheimer, A. (2009). Everything old is new again: Applying defined benefit solutions to defined contribution programs. *Benefits Quarterly, 26*(1), 38–40.

Gramlich, E. M. (1990). *A guide to benefit-cost analysis* (2nd ed.). Long Grove, IL: Prentice Hall.

Gramlich, E. M. (1996). Different approaches for dealing with social security. *The American Economic Review, 86,* 358–362. doi:10.1257/jep.10.3.55

Gran, B. (2008). Shifts in public–private provision of retirement income: A four-country comparison. *Research on Aging, 30,* 507–543. doi:10.1177/0164027508319657

Grech, A. G. (2007). Pension policy in EU25 and its impact on pension benefits. *Benefits Quarterly, 15*(3), 299–311.

Green, D., Palmquist, B., & Schickler, E. (2002). *Partisan hearts and minds: Political parties and the social identities of voters.* New Haven, CT: Yale University Press.

Gruber, J., & Wise, D. (1997). *Social Security programs and retirement around the world* (NBER Working Paper No. 9407). Cambridge, MA: National Bureau of Economic Research.

Guillaud, E. (2008). *Preferences for redistribution: A European comparative analysis* (Paris School of Economics Working Paper No. 2008-41). Retrieved from http://www.iza.org/conference_files/SUMS2007/guillaud_e3355.pdf

Gustman, A. L., & Steinmar, T. L. (2002). *The Social Security early entitlement age in a structural model of retirement and wealth* (University of Michigan Retirement Research Center Working Paper No. 2002-029). Retrieved from http://www.mrrc.isr.umich.edu/publications/papers/pdf/wp029.pdf

Hakim, C. (1987). *Research design: Strategies and choices in the design of social research.* London, England: Allen & Unwin.

Hall, P., & Soskice, D. (2001). *Varieties of capitalism: The institutional foundations of comparative advantage.* Oxford, England: Oxford University Press.

Hieger, M., & Shipman, W. (1997). *Common objections to a market-based social security system: A response* (SSP No. 10). Retrieved from http://www.cato.org/pubs/ssps/ssp10es.html

Hines, J. R., & Taylor, T. (2005). Shortfalls in the long run: Predictions about the Social Security trust fund. *Journal of Economic Perspectives, 19*(2), 3–9. doi:10.1257/0895330054048759

Hogg, B. J. (2009). The tides of retirement: Navigating the sea of change in DC plan. *Benefits Quarterly, 25*(1), 7–10. Retrieved from http://www.aon.com/attachments/thought-leadership/Sea_Change_DC_Plans.pdf

Holder, R. (2009). Defined contribution plan: Design in a post-PPA environment. *Benefits Quarterly, 25*(1), 11–16.

Howe, N., & Jackson, R. (1998, June 15). *The myth of the 2.2 percent solution* (SSP Paper No. 11). Retrieved from http://www.cato.org/publications/social-security-choice-paper/myth-22-percent-solution

Imarhiagbe, N. (2014). *Future sustainability of Social Security trends in unemployment and retirement benefits* (Doctoral dissertation). Available from ProQuest Dissertations and Theses database. (UMI No. 3615999)

Johnson, R. (2005). *Older Americans' economic security: Working longer to enhance retirement security.* Washington, DC: Urban Institute.

Kamenir, J. (2009). How to make defined benefit pension plans attractive to 21st century employers. *Benefits Quarterly, 25*(1), 51–56.

Kastner, S., & Rector, C. (2005). Partisanship and the path to financial openness. *Comparative Political Studies, 38*, 484–506. doi:10.1177/0010414004272540

Kay, S. J., & Kritzer, B. E. (2001). Social security in Latin America: Recent reforms and challenges. *Economic Review, 86*(1). Retrieved from https://www.frbatlanta.org/-/media/Documents/research/publications/economic-review/2001/vol86no1_kay-kritzer.pdf?laen

Kegler, C. M., Rigler, J., & Honeycutt, S. (2010). How does community context influence coalitions in the formation stage? A multiple case study based on the community coalition action theory. *BMC Public Health*, Art. 10. doi:10.1186/1471-2458-10-90

Kennelly, B. B. (2005). Myths and realities about Social Security and privatization. *Generations, 29*(1), 97–99.

Kilgour, J. G. (2009). The pension plan funding debate and PPA of 2006. *Benefits Quarterly, 23*(4), 7–20.

Kitao, S. (2011). *Sustainable Social Security: Four options* (Report No. 505). New York, NY: Federal Reserve Bank of New York.

Klein, J. (2006). The history of public and private social policy in the United States. *Canadian Review of American Studies, 36*(2), 237–241.

Knoke, D., Bohrnstedt, G. W., & Mee, A. P. (2002). *Statistics from social data analysis* (4th ed.). Sydney, Australia: Thomson & Wadsworth.

Kohn, L. T. (1997). *Methods in case study analysis* (Technical Publication No. 2). Washington, DC: The Center for Studying Health System Change. Retrieved from http://www.hschange.com/CONTENT/158/158.pdf

Korczyk, S. M. (2005). Women's issues in individual social security accounts: Chile, Australia and the United Kingdom. *Benefits Quarterly, 21*(3), 37–47.

Kosterlitz, J. (2006). Private accounts for Democrats. *National Journal, 38*(49), 60–61.

Kumar, M. (2007). Mixed methodology research design in educational technology. *Alberta Journal of Educational Research, 53*(1), 34–44.

Layman, G. C., & Carsey, T. M. (2002). Party polarization and "conflict extension" in the American electorate. *American Journal of Political Science, 46,* 786–802. doi:10.2307/3088434

Leidy, M. (1997). *Investing U.S. Social Security Trust Fund assets in private securities* (IMF Working Paper WP/97/112). Washington, DC: International Monetary Fund.

Lessard, C., Contandriopoulos, A. P., & Beaulieu, M. D. (2009). The role of economic evaluation in the decision-making process of family physicians: Design and methods of a qualitative embedded multiple-case study. *BMC Family Practice,* Art. 10. doi:10.1186/1471-2296-10-15

Lijphart, A. (1999). *Pattern of democracy: Government forms and performance in thirty-six countries.* New Haven, CT: Yale University Press.

Lips, C. (1998). *The working poor and social security privatization: Restoring the opportunity to save* (Briefing Paper No. 40). Retrieved from http://www.cato.org/publications/briefing-paper/working-poor-social-security-privatization-restoring-opportunity-save

Lips, C. (1999). *State and local government retirement programs: Lessons in alternatives to Social Security* (SSP Choice Paper No. 16). Retrieved from http://www.cato.org/publications/social-security-choice-paper/state-local-government-retirement-programs-lessons-alternatives-social-security

Lowenstein, R. (2008, May 4). Entitled to what? To the next president: There is a retirement crisis coming. *The New York Times.* Retrieved from http://www.nytimes.com/2008/05/04/magazine/04wwln-lede-t.html

MaCurdy, T. E., & Shoven., J. B. (1999). *Asset allocation and risk allocation: Can Social Security improve its future solvency problems by investing in private securities?* (NBER Working Paper No. 7015). Cambridge, MA: National Bureau of Economic Research.

Madhavan, A., & Ming, K. (2002). *The hidden costs of index rebalancing: A case study of the S&P 500 composition changes of July 19, 2002.* New York, NY: ITG. Retrieved from http://www.itg.com/news_events/papers/sandpindexchange.pdf

Marmor, T. R., & Mashaw, J. L. (2006). Understanding social insurance: Fairness, affordability, and the 'modernization' of Social Security and Medicare. *Health Affairs, 25,* w114–w134. doi:10.1377/hlthaff.25.w114

Maroney, J. J., Jackson, C. M., Rupert, T. J., & Zhang, Y. (2011). The effect of accounting information on taxpayers' acceptance of tax reform. T*he Journal of the American Taxation Association, 34*(1), 113–135.

Marshall, V. W. (1999). Reasoning with case studies: Issues of an aging workforce. *Journal of Aging Studies, 13,* 377–389. doi:10.1016/S0890-4065(99)00016-X

Martin, P. P. (2004). Comparing replacement rates under private and federal retirement system. *Social Security Bulletin, 65*(1). Retrieved from https://www.ssa.gov/policy/docs/ssb/v65n1/v65n1p17.html

MassBudget. (2011). *Workforce characteristics and wages in the public and private sectors.* Boston, MA: Massachusetts Budget and Policy Center. Retrieved from http://massbudget.org/report_window.php?loc=Compensation_3_11.html

Mastrobuoni, G. (2006). *Labor supply effects of the recent Social Security benefit cuts: Empirical estimates using cohort discontinuities.* Retrieved from https://www.princeton.edu/ceps/workingpapers/136mastrobuoni.pdf

Matijascic, M., & Kay, S. J. (2006). Social Security at the crossroads: Toward effective pension reform in Latin America. *International Social Security Review, 59*(1), 3–26. doi:10.1111/j.1468-246X.2006.00231.x

Mayer, C. (2009). Helping retirees maximize sustainable income. *Benefits Quarterly, 25*(1), 41–48.

McHale, J. (1999). *The risk of Social Security benefit rule changes: Some international evidence* (NBER Working Paper No. 7031). Cambridge, MA: National Bureau of Economic Research.

McNabb, D. E. (2002). *Research methods in public administration and nonprofit management: Quantitative and qualitative approaches.* Armonk, ME: Sharpe.

McNabb, J., Timmons, D., Song, J., & Puckett, C. (2009). Uses of administrative data at the Social Security Administration. *Social Security Bulletin, 69*(1). Retrieved from https://www.ssa.gov/policy/docs/ssb/v69n1/v69n1p75.html

Meltzer, A. H., & Richard, S. F. (1981). A rational theory of the size of government. *The Journal of Political Economy, 89,* 914–927. doi:10.1086/261013

Merriam, L. (1946). *Relief and Social Security.* Washington, DC: The Brookings Institution.

Merriam, S. B. (1989). *Qualitative research and case study applications in education.* San Francisco, CA: Jossey-Bass.

Mesa-Lago, C. (2007). Social security in Latin America: Pension and health care reforms in the last quarter century. *Latin American Research Review, 42*(2), 182–201. doi:10.1353/lar.2007.0024.

Meyer, C. W. (1987). *Social Security: A critical of radical reform proposals.* Lexington, MA: D. C. Health.

Midgley, J., & Tang, K. (2002). Individualism, collectivism and the marketization of social security: Chile and China compared. *Review of Policy Research, 19,* 57–84. doi:10.1111/j.1541-1338.2002.tb00296.x/enhancedabs

Moore, M. (2003, January 16). *Social Security and stock market risk* (no. 429). Washington, DC: National Center for Policy Analysis. Retrieved from http:www.ncpa.org/pub/ba/ba429

Mueller, D., & Murrell, P. (1986). Interest groups and the size of government. *Public Choice, 48,* 125–145. doi:10.1007/BF00179727

Muller, L. A., Moore, J. H., Jr., & Elliott, K. R. (2009). Who is likely to opt out of an automatic enrollment plan? Who is likely to stay in? *Benefit Quarterly, 25*(1), 47–62.

Mulligan, C. B., & Sala-I-Martin, X. (1999). *Social Security in theory and practice (I): Facts and political theories* (NBER Work Paper No. 7118). Cambridge, MA: National Bureau of Economic Research.

Mundell, R. A. (1960). The monetary dynamics of international adjustment under fixed and flexible exchange rates. *The Quarterly Journal of Economics, 74*, 227–257. doi:10.2307/1884252

Munnell, A. H. (1977). *The future of Social Security*. Washington, DC: The Brookings Institution.

Myers, R. J. (1975). Social Security: Homewood, IL: R. D. Irwin.

Nadler, J. (1999). Securing Social Security. *The Washington Quarterly, 22*(1), 185–187. doi:10.1080/01636609909550377

Neuman, L. (2005). *Social research methods: Qualitative and quantitative approaches* (6th ed.). Boston, MA: Allyn & Bacon.

Newberry, J. (2002). It may be time to stock up. *ABA Journal, 88*(5), 58.

Olson, M. (1965). *The logic of collective action*. Cambridge MA: Harvard University Press.

O'Neil, J. (2002, April 9). *The trust fund, the surplus, and the real Social Security problem* (Social Security Choice Paper No. 26). Retrieved from http://www.cato.org/publications/social-security-choice-paper/trust-fund-surplus-real-social-security-problem

Ostaszewski, K. M. (1997). *Privatizing the Social Security trust fund? Don't let the government invest* (Social Security Choice Paper No. 6). Retrieved from http://www.cato.org/publications/social-security-choice-paper/privatizing-social-security-trust-fund-dont-let-government-invest

Papke, L. E. (2004). Pension plan choice in the public sector: The case of Michigan employees. *National Tax Journal, 2*(57), 8–27.

Pechman, J. A., Aaron, H. J., & Taussig, M. K. (1968). *Social Security: Perspectives for reform*. Washington, DC: The Brookings Institution.

Perotti, R. (1996). Growth, income distribution, and democracy: What the data say. *Journal of Economic Growth, 1*, 149–187. doi:10.1007/BF00138861

Peters, G. B. (2005). I'm ok, You're (not) ok: The private welfare state in the United States. *Social Policy & Administration, 39,* 166–180. doi:10.1111/j.1467-9515.2005.00432.x

Podsakoff, P. M., MacKenzie, S. B., Lee, J., & Podsakoff, N. (2003). Common method biases in behavioral research: A critical review of the literature and recommendation remedies. *Journal of Applied Psychology, 88,* 879–903. doi:10.1037/0021-9010.88.5.879

Queisser, M., & Whitehouse, E. (2006). Comparing the pension promises of 30 OECD counties. *International Social Security Review, 59*(3), 49–77. doi:10.1111/j.1468-246X.2006.00247.x

Quinn, D. P., & Inclán, C. (1997). The origins of financial openness: A study of current and capital account liberalization. *American Journal of Political Science, 41,* 771–813. doi:1.2307/2111675

Reinsdorf, M. B., & Lenze, D. G. (2009). Research spotlight: Defined benefit pensions and household income and wealth. *Survey of Current Business, August,* 50–62.

Reno, V. P. (2005). How Social Security works. *Generations, 29*(1), 23–26.

Report of the President's Commission. (2001, December). *Strengthening Social Security and creating personnel wealth for Americans.* Retrieved from http://govinfo.library.unt.edu/csss/reports/Final_report.pdf

Richtman, M. (2001, December 11). *Press conference with the Executive Director.* Washington, DC: National Committee to Preserve Social Security and Medicare.

Robertson, (1985). Is the current Social Security program: Financially feasible in the long run? *Benefits Quarterly, 1985*(3), 36–42.

Rodriguez, J. (1999, July 30). *Chile's private pension system at 18: Its current state and future challenges* (Social Security Choice Paper No. 17). Retrieved from http://www.cato.org/publications/social-security-choice-paper/chiles-private-pension-system-18-its-current-state-future-challenges

Rogot, E., Sorlie, P. D., & Johnson, N. J. (1992, July–August). Life expectancy by employment status, income, and education in the National Longitudinal Mortality Study. *Public Health Reports, 107,* 457–461.

Rohter, L. (2008, August 13). Social security too hot to touch? Not in 2008. *The New York Times,* A20. Retrieved from http://www.nytimes.com/2008/08/14/us/politics/14retire.html?sq=

Rounds, C. E., Jr. (2000). *Property rights: The hidden issue of Social Security reform* (Social Security Choice Paper No. 19). Retrieved from http://www.cato.org/publications/social-security-choice-paper/property-rights-hidden-issue-social-security-reform

Rowley, J. (2002). Using case studies in research. *Management Research News, 23,* 16–27. doi:10.1108/01409170210782990

Rudnick, L. P., Smith, J. E., & Rubin, R. L. (2005). *American identities: An introductory textbook.* Hoboken, NJ: Wiley-Blackwell.

Sanders, D. S. (1973). *The impact of the reform movements on social policy change: The case of social insurance.* Fair Lawn, NJ: R. E. Burdick.

Sanders, D. H., Murph, A. F., & Eng, R. J. (1980). *Statistics: A fresh approach* (2nd ed.). New York, NY: McGraw-Hill.

Saving, T. R. (2006). Perspective: Social insurance and elderly entitlement reform: Are they compatible? *Health Affairs, 25,* 138–140. doi:10.1377/hlthaff.25.w138

Schulz, J., Carrin, G., Krupp, H., Peschke, M., Sclar, E., & Steenberge, J. V. (1974). *Providing adequate retirement income: Pension reform in the United States and abroad.* Hanover, NH: Brandeis University Press.

Schulz, J. H., & Gorin, S. (2005). Let's not gamble with Social Security. *Health & Social Work, 30,* 75. doi:10.1093/hsw/30.1.75

Shaw, G., M., & Mysiewicz, S. E. (2006). The polls—Trends: Social Security and Medicare. *Public Opinion Quarterly, 68,* 394–423. doi:10.1093/poq/nfh033

Shipman, W. G. (1995). *Retiring with dignity: Social Security vs. private markets* (Social Security Choice Paper No. 2). Retrieved from http://www.cato.org/publications

/social-security-choice-paper/retiring-dignity-social-security-vs-private-markets

Shipman, W. G. (2003). *Retirement finance reform issues facing the European Union* (SSP No. 28). Retrieved from http://www.cato.org/pubs/ssps/ssp-28es.html

Siems, T. F. (2001). *Reengineering Social Security in the new economy* (SSP No. 22). Retrieved from http://www.cato.org/pubs/ssps/ssp-22es.html

Singleton, R., Jr., & Straits, B. C. (1999). *Approaches to social research* (3rd ed.). New York, NY: Oxford University Press.

Sjoblom, K. (1985). Voting for social security. *Public Choice, 45*, 225–240. doi:10.1007/BF00124021

Social Security Administration. (2003). *Fast facts & figures about Social Security*. Retrieved from https://www.socialsecurity.gov/policy/docs/chartbooks/fast_facts/2003/fast_facts03.html

Social Security Administration. (2006, April 18). *Analytic issue*. Retrieved from http://www.ssa.gov/regulations/index.htm

Social Security Administration. (2007). *How your benefit is figured*. Retrieved from http://www.socialsecurity.gov/mystatement/howfigured.htm

Social Security Administration. (2009a). *Provisions affecting retirement age*. Retrieved from http://www.ssa.gov/OACT/solvency/provisions/retireage.html.

Social Security Administration. (2009b). *Understanding the benefits*. Retrieved from https://www.ssa.gov/pubs/EN-05-10024.pdf

Social Security Administration, Office of Policy. (2000). *Fast facts about Social Security*. Retrieved from https://www.ssa.gov/policy/docs/chartbooks/fast_facts/

Social Security Administration, Office of Policy. (2007). *Fast facts & figures about Social Security*. Retrieved from https://www.ssa.gov/policy/docs/chartbooks/fast_facts/

Social Security Advisory Board. (July 2001). *Social Security: Why action should be taken soon.* Retrieved from http://ssab.gov/Portals/0/Documents/Sooner_Later_2010.pdf

Song, J., & Manchester, J. (2007). Have people delayed claiming retirement benefits? Responses to change in social security rules. *Social Security Bulletin, 67*(20), 20–23. Retrieved from https://www.ssa.gov/policy/docs/ssb/v67n2/v67n2p1.pdf

Stark, A. Folbre, N., & Shaw, L. B. (Eds.). (2005). Explorations gender and aging: Cross-national contrasts. *Feminist Economics, 11*(2), 163–197. doi:10.1080/13545700500115985

Steinberg, A., & Lucas, L. (2004). Shifting responsibility to workers: The future of retirement adequacy in the United States. *Benefits Quarterly, 20*(4), 15–26.

Steuerle, C. E., Carasso, A., & Cohen, L. (2004). *How progressive is Social Security and why?* Washington, DC: Urban Institute.

Streeck, W. (2009). *Re-forming capitalism: Institutional change in the German political economy.* Oxford, England: Oxford University Press.

Sutton, T. D. (2005). Economic justice and the future of Social Security. *Human Rights, 32*(2). Retrieved from http://www.americanbar.org/publications/human_rights_magazine_home/human_rights_vol32_2005/summer2005/hr_summer05_socsec.html

Svihula, J., & Estes, C. L. (2008). Social Security privatization: An ideologically structured movement. *The Journal of Sociology & Social Welfare, 35*(1), 75–104. http://scholarworks.wmich.edu/cgi/viewcontent.cgi?article=3316&context=jssw

Tabellini, G. (2000). A positive theory of social security. *Scandinavian Journal of Economics, 102,* 523–545. doi:10.1111/1467-9442.00213

Tanner, M. (2000). *"Saving" Social Security is not enough* (Social Security Choice Paper No. 20). Retrieved from http://www.cato.org/publications/social-security-choice-paper/saving-social-security-is-not-enough

Tanner, M. D. (2002). *No second best: The unappetizing alternatives to social security privatization* (Social Security Choice Paper No. 24). Retrieved from http://www.cato.org/publications/social-security-choice-paper/no-second-best-unappetizing-alternatives-social-security-privatization

Tanner, M. (2003). *The better deal: Estimating rates of return under a system of individual accounts* (Social Security Choice Paper No. 31). Retrieved from http://www.cato.org/publications/social-security-choice-paper/better-deal-estimating-rates-return-under-system-individual-accounts

Tucker, M. (2002). Partial privatization of Social Security: A simulation of possible outcomes and risks to workers. *Financial Services Review, 11,* 311–326.

Turner, J. (2005, March 11). Individual accounts: Lessons from Sweden. *International Social Security Review, 57*(1), 65–84. doi:10.1111/j.0020-871x.2004.00181.x

Updegrave, W. (2005). Who says we can't handle private accounts? *Money Magazine, 34*(4), 78–80.

U.S. Board of Trustees of the Federal Old Age and Survivors Insurance and Disability Insurance Trust Funds. (2001). *The 2001 annual report of the board of trustees of the federal old-age and survivors insurance and federal disability insurance trust funds.* Retrieved from http://www.ssa.gov/OACT/TR/TR04/II_project.html

U.S. Board of Trustees of the Federal Old Age and Survivors Insurance and Disability Insurance Trust Funds. (2004). *The 2004 annual report of the board of trustees of the federal old-age and survivors insurance and federal disability insurance trust funds.* Retrieved from http://www.ssa.gov/OACT/TR/TR04/II_project.html Social Security

U.S. Board of Trustees of the Federal Old Age and Survivors Insurance and Disability Insurance Trust Funds. (2009). *The 2009 annual report of the board of trustees of the federal old-age and survivors insurance and federal disability insurance trust funds.* Retrieved from https://www.hathitrust.org/usdocs_registry/catalog/0dc9b0e5-2a73-4f5e-9b29-7c8a00ff9a7c

Vandersanden, R. (2009). New strategies for DB plan management. *Benefits Quarterly, 24*(4), 36–41.

Walter, S. (2010). Globalization and the welfare state. Testing the micro foundations of the compensation hypothesis. *International Studies Quarterly, 54*, 403–426. doi:10.1111/j.1468-2478.2010.00593.x

Weaver, C. L. (1982). *The crisis in Social Security: Economic and political origins.* Durham, NC: Duke University Press.

Weller, C. E. (2005). *Social Security privatization: The retirement savings gamble.* Washington, DC: Center for American Progress. Retrieved from https://cdn.americanprogress.org/wp-content/uploads/kf/ss_gambling_weller.pdf

Weller, C. E. (2006). Social Security privatization and market risk. *Review of Policy Research, 23*, 531–546. doi:10.1111/j.1541-1338.2006.00214.x

Weller, C. E. (2007). Pure: A proposal for more retirement income security. *Journal of Aging & Social Policy, 19*, 21–38. doi:10.1300/J031v19n01_02

Weller, C. E., & Bragg, M. (2002). T.I.N.A: There is no alternative to social security. *Social Policy, 32*(2), 61–66.

Whitman, D., & Purcell, P. (2006). Topics in aging: Income and poverty among older Americans in 2005. *Benefits Quarterly, 22*(4), 48–61.

Zach, L. (2006). Using a multiple-case studies design to investigate the information-seeking behavior of arts administrators. *Library Trends, 55*, 4–21. doi:10.1353/lib.2006.0055

Zogby, J., Bonacci, R., Bruce, J., Daley, D., & Wittman, R. (2003, January 6). *Public opinion and private accounts: Measuring risk and confidence in rethinking Social Security* (Social Security Choice Paper No. 29). Retrieved http://www.cato.org/publications/social-security-choice-paper/public-opinion-private-accounts-measuring-risk-confidence-rethinking-social-security

GLOSSARY

Buyers	Those who carry out the formal arrangements for purchase, service, delivery, and financial terms.
Compensatory decision rule	A type of decision rule for evaluating alternatives where consumers consider each brand with respect to how it performs on relevant or salient attributes and the importance of each attribute. This decision rule allows for a negative evaluation or performance on a particular attribute to be compensated for by a positive evaluation on another attribute.
Compensatory model	A model which assumes that consumers judge a limited number of product attributes, that the attributes vary in importance to the consumer, and that strength in one area compensates for weakness in another
Competitive advantage	The part of a firm's total offering which is superior to that of its
Competitors	Something unique or special that a firm does or possesses that provides an advantage over its competitors

Consumer markets	The most visible markets, which consist of individual customers who buy products for their own use or for use by other members of their households
Core benefit	The need that a product fulfills or the problem it solves
Customer satisfaction	the extent to which a product's perceived performance matches a buyer's expectations. If the product's performance falls short of expectations, the buyer is dissatisfied. If performance matches or exceeds expectations, the buyer is satisfied or delighted
Demand	A relation among the various amounts of a product that buyers would be willing and able to purchase at possible alternative prices during a given period of time, all other remaining the same
Demands	Human wants that are backed by buying power
De-marketing	Marketing to reduce demand temporarily or permanently; the aim is not to destroy demand, but only to reduce or shift it
Horizontal markets	Markets on which products are sold to a wide range of industries
Market	The set of all actual and potential buyers of a product or service
Marketing	A social and managerial process whereby individuals and groups obtain what they need and want through creating and exchanging products and value with others
Marketing concept	The philosophy that business organizations achieve their profit and other goals by satisfying consumers

Marketing environment	The actors and forces outside marketing that affect marketing management's ability to develop and maintain successful transactions with its target customers
Marketing information system	People, equipment, and procedures to gather, sort, analyze. Evaluate, and distribute needed, timely, and accurate information to marketing decision makers
Marketing intelligence	Everyday information about developments in the marketing environment that helps managers prepare and adjust marketing plans
Marketing management	The analysis, planning, implementation, and control of programs designed to create, build, and maintain beneficial exchanges with target buyers for the purpose of achieving organizational objectives
Marketing research	The systematic design, collection, analysis, and reporting of data relevant to a specific marketing situation facing an organization
Non-compensatory model	A model of information processing in which a high rating for one attribute does not offset a low rating for other
Product	anything that can be offered to a market for attention, acquisition, use, or consumption that might satisfy a want or need. It includes physical objects, services, persons, places, organizations, and ideas
Service	any activity or benefit that one party can offer to another that is essentially intangible and does not result in the ownership of anything

Service market	All organizations that buy in order to produce services
Social marketing (or cause marketing)	The design, implementation, and control of marketing programs calculated to influence the acceptability of social ideas.

OPERATIONAL DEFINITIONS

Alternative plans to Social Security: different ways of providing retirement benefits to workers (Matijascic & Kay, 2006).

Individual private account: a retirement system designed to allow workers to contribute to individual retirement savings accounts (Reinsdorf & Lenze, 2009).

Parallel: a new private retirement system introduced by Colombia and Peru to compete with their public systems without dismantling current plans (Weller, 2006).

Social Security privatization: is a plan that allows individuals to invest a portion of their payroll taxes into private savings accounts (Weller, 2006).

Substitute: a public retirement system that was replaced by a private plan to provide benefits to retired workers (Matijascic & Kay, 2006).

Supplemental Pension Savings Plan (SPSP): this is a mandatory defined-contribution plan introduced by cities, to replace Social Security for city employees (Dattalo, 2007).

Defined contribution: retirement benefits are provided based on the amount of money that has been accumulated in workers' accounts (Reinsdorf & Lenze, 2009).

Defined benefit: workers' benefits are calculated based on their length of service and average or final pay (Reinsdorf & Lenze, 2009).

THE AUTHOR

Dr. Napoleon Imarhiagbe is also the authors of Managing Public Organization Through Leadership: Bottom- Up-Leadership and Future Sustainability of Social Security Trends in Higher Unemployment and Retirement Benefits.

Dr. Imarhiagbe is an expert in public management and a trained administrator. He has a bachelor's degree in Public Administration from Medgar Evers College of the City University of New York (CUNY). He earned a Master of Public Administration (MPA) from John Jay College of Criminal Justice CUNY with a specialization in Management and Operations. He graduated with distinction from the prestigious Walden University School of Public Management with a Ph.D. in Public Policy and Administration.